RECLAIM

PRAISE

Hymns
from a
Spiritual
Journey

ANDREW PRATT

STAINER & BELL

First published in 2006 by
Stainer & Bell Limited, PO Box 110, Victoria House, 23 Gruneisen Road,
London N3 1DZ, England.

Cover illustration: Acrylic on cloth by Jonathan Pratt (1976–1999)

British Library Cataloguing-in-Publication Data
A catalogue record of this book is available from the British Library

ISBN: 978 0 85249 891 0

Printed in Great Britain by Caligraving Ltd, Thetford

Contents

~~~~~~~~~

Hymns from a Spiritual Journey

In the beginning

Covenant relationship with God

Which allowed lament

And still allows lament

In lives of worship

In lives of justice

Going into all the world

Longing to praise again

Foreword

Why, one might wonder, is a Presbyterian woman who teaches religion at a small college in the southern Appalachians writing the foreword to a collection of hymns by a Methodist minister and tutor in contextual theology at Hartley Victoria College in Manchester, England? A couple of answers might suggest themselves to the careful reader. For example, Andrew Pratt prefaces his hymn text 'See the glory of the morning' (No. 4) by noting how the changing colours of autumnal leaves take him in memory to North Carolina; five of the hymns in this collection were written at a place not an hour from my home: the retreat centre at Lake Junaluska, where in October 2003 he attended an Academy of Global Song, sponsored by the Board of Global Ministries of the United Methodist Church. Yet, I note with some sadness that I was not even aware he was in the neighbourhood for that event three years ago; had I known, I would surely have driven the short distance for an opportunity to meet him.

For, we have never met – at least, not face to face. So a next possible hypothesis arises to account for this foreword by an admitted stranger. Andrew Pratt mentions that his text 'Lives are the currency spent in war's carnage' (No. 71) was recipient of an 'Honorable Mention' from The Hymn Society in the US and Canada. Might the Hymn Society on this side of the Atlantic prove the link between us? Here, the connection comes much closer to the truth. I did not even know of Andrew Pratt when we both had texts selected by the Society for publication after the events of 11 September 2001 (I was relatively new to hymnology at the time). However, when his collection *Whatever Name or Creed* was published by Stainer & Bell in 2002, I was asked to write a review of it for *The Hymn*, the professional journal of the Hymn Society on this continent.

It was then that I became a fan. In that review, I wrote (among other laudatory appraisals): 'Unflinchingly honest, Pratt's poetry speaks in voices ranging from tender to outraged, lyrical to caustic. Among his strongest texts are those that startle with sharp juxtapositions, refusing to let us rest in the merely "pretty".' A similar assessment applies to the current collection. For example, 'The doors are closed, the music hushed' (No. 94) begins with an image of the solemnity of worship, but moves quickly to name the travesty that arises when a congregation locks its doors (literally or metaphorically) to outsiders, turning a deaf ear to the cries of those 'beyond [the] walls'. Or, in a pointed response to witless political rhetoric relating to an alleged 'axis of evil' (No. 100), he writes simply, 'Evil has no axis/ outside the human mind.' The quicker we are to label and condemn others, he suggests, the more we condemn ourselves with our own self-righteousness. Those who have ears to hear, let them hear.

It is not just Andrew Pratt's prophetic honesty that appeals to me. It is also his wrestling with ways to keep the faith claims of a 2000-year-old religion credible within the thought-worlds of the modern day. Not many writers of hymn texts have received an extensive training in the natural sciences, for example; yet he was on his way to completing a doctorate in fish pharmacology when he changed course and opted instead to train for the Methodist ministry. His ease with scientific vocabulary is fully evident in the odes to cosmic creation that open this volume, singing of the 'pan-galactic breath of God' (No. 1), and of 'stellar collisions ... at the birthing of matter and time' (No. 2). His scientist's penchant for questioning also infuses his language of lament. In the aftermath of the tsunami of 2004, Pratt voiced the anguished question: Was God 'midwife at the birth' (No. 22) of the tidal wave that swept away so many lives? He refuses, though, to offer pieties by way of reply. Rather, he lets the question stand in all its starkness, pleading not so much for a vindication of God's ways, as an indication of God's redemptive presence:

> God, come and join your people in
> the centre of their loss.
> If you are real then show yourself
> upon this present cross.   *(No. 22)*

This text is one that I featured in a presentation on lament delivered as part of the Erik Routley Lectures in Congregational Song at a conference of the Presbyterian Association of Musicians in the summer of 2005. I used it again in an article on hymnic treatments of the theodicy of so-called 'natural evil', published in the winter 2006 edition of *The Hymn*. By the time I had contacted Andrew Pratt with a second or third request for permission to quote from his words, I suppose he realised I was enough of a fan to ask me to write this foreword.

Agreeing to his request gave me the privilege of an early read-through of the complete collection. From the table of contents, which stands as an appealingly-written outline of the journey of faith, to the commentaries that run as a narrative thread throughout the volume and are as much worth studying as the hymns themselves, I found myself caught up in the storyline. Near the very end appears a text that eloquently speaks to the volume's title:

> Light is dawning on the future,
> guiding us within this maze;
> love and grace will hold and nurture,
> forming faith, reclaiming praise.   *(No. 146)*

Drawn by such a vision, readers will experience this volume as a pilgrimage, and Andrew Pratt as an engaging companion. With him, we sing as we go.

MARY LOUISE BRINGLE   October 2006
Chair of the Humanities Division, Brevard College, NC
President-elect of The Hymn Society in the US and Canada

Preface

The background to this collection is my experience of trying to reclaim the capacity to praise God since the death of my son in 1999.

In doing this two things have emerged. I first began to write hymns to help me to understand and make sense of theology as I prepared for ministry. My background had been in science and a lot of what I was struggling with made little sense. Since then I have always returned to verse when attempting to understand something complicated, or to communicate it in a more simple or memorable fashion. Also, I have found myself mapping my pilgrimage. Sydney Carter's creed 'Nothing fixed or final' makes sense to me. Faith grows in a haphazard way. Strong convictions are formed, only to be overturned by circumstance. The shards of our belief are scattered, and we struggle to find all the fragments, let alone to put them back together. Then what we have is at best distorted, or at worst unrecognisable. But is that really worse? Perhaps it is more truthfully a sign that we are struggling with the infinite, relating to the divine. We are like children presented with an immense jigsaw puzzle, way beyond our capacity to solve, and the struggle is made more difficult because the pictures on the pieces are not all present. Perhaps we do not even have all the pieces. And we begin to wonder who does, and are shocked to find them possessed by people we have disregarded or despised.

This personal theology has not developed in an orderly fashion, and so to present the texts chronologically would be confusing. Instead, each text will stand on its own without explanation. However, should you wish to join me on my pilgrimage, then my story will take you from the Old Testament through to the New Testament, mirroring both my Christian experience and a journey begun in the early 1970s and continuing to the present day.

I am grateful to Damian Boddy, who continues to provide help for me with music, and to Marjorie Dobson, who has offered her critique of my words. As ever I am responsible for the final choices.

ANDREW PRATT   June 2006

Hymns from a Spiritual Journey

Whispers rippled through the cosmos,
pan–galactic breath of God;
marking paths of whirling planets,
stellar strings where stars first trod.
Major chords of constellations
ringing on the staves of time,
move toward a sombre minor:
music for creation's rhyme.

God is in this wild confusion
bringing order, giving grace;
author, ground of all creation,
fount of being, Lord of space.
All transcendent power and glory
now distilled, condensed, confined;
shaped while shaping rich resources
cradling waiting humankind.

Metre: 8.7.8.7.D.

Suggested Tunes: BETHANY (Smart) and HOLY MANNA

Looking back over the hymns I have written is, for me, like looking at a diary. The words chronicle my life. In 1999 my son was killed in a road accident. That shakes your faith, if it doesn't destroy it. Praise becomes dry and dead on your lips. I've tried to reclaim praise, to make sense of God again. This has taken me back not only to the beginning of the Bible, but also to the starting point of my faith.

In the beginning I was moved by the beauty of seas and mountains, trees and sunsets. I sought explanations for the wonder I saw and felt, and was pushed beyond my scientific training and understanding. I still try to make theological sense of these experiences, which often, as in the case of this hymn, inspire me to write. During 2004, it was reported that astronomers had recaptured the sounds of the early universe, showing it was born, not with a bang, but a quiet whisper that became a dull roar. Over the first million years, the music of the cosmos changed from a bright major chord to a sombre minor one.

When my faith was being born, I began to explore art, music and poetry. I took the first faltering steps towards a belief in God and found that those steps of faith were affirmed. I own a telescope and continue to be amazed by the cosmos, the immensity and wonder of creation.

God-given energy, flaring and fiery,
stellar collisions of fury and pace;
shafts of the light from the cosmic conception
beaming to earth from infinity's space.

Stars for millennia driven by forces
formed at the birthing of matter and time;
mystical sinews restraining the planets,
elegant science and God's hidden rhyme.

These are the visions of wonder and rapture,
signs of significance, pointers to place,
drawing us out from our narrow discernment,
windows to love and God's infinite grace.

Metre: 11.10.11.10.

Suggested Tune: IN THE BEGINNING GOD PLAYED WITH THE PLANETS

I developed an understanding of how God was behind the wonder that I was beginning to experience and explore. I didn't know it at the time, but I was sharing something of the 'mysterium et tremendum' – mystery and awe – spoken of by Rudolf Otto in another generation. I was tapping into a rich vein of theological tradition and interpretation.

IN THE BEGINNING GOD PLAYED WITH THE PLANETS

David Lee (1956–)

Lyrics (underlaid in the music):

God-giv-en e-ner-gy, flar - ing and fi - ery,
stel - lar col-li-sions of fu - ry and pace;_
shafts of the light from the
cos-mic con-cep - tion_ beam-ing to earth from in-fi - ni-ty's space._

3　This hazy, gleaming veil

This hazy, gleaming veil,
this cloudy, milky skein,
this cosmic raft of swirling space –
how can we be so vain?

A hundred-billion stars
form that galactic space,
these myriad sparks of dancing light
are signings of God's grace.

This place of hopes and dreams
God gives into our hands,
and we are stewards of its worth,
its rich majestic strands.

So limited our grasp,
so narrow human scope,
so much is still beyond our reach,
yet beauty frames our hope.

Metre: SM

Suggested Tunes: GARELOCHSIDE and DENNIS

I continue to wonder. The nearest star, apart from the sun, is some 4.2 light years away; the distance that light travels in a year (it travels at 186,000 miles a second) times 4.2. The distances are immense.

We are beginning to understand the practicalities of the responsibility placed on us as stewards of this creation, spoken of poetically in Psalm 8. An article about our galaxy, the Milky Way, published in the January 2004 issue of 'Scientific American', inspired this text.

In the beginning

4   See the glory of the morning

See the glory of the morning:
autumn leaves of red and gold;
flashing silver sea, and sunlight,
new each dawning, never old.

God is painting from a palette
each kaleidoscopic scene,
visions that we greet with wonder,
shot with crimson, streaked with green.

Every sight and sound is different,
every new epiphany
points to God's eternal glory,
fires our joyous litany.

Metre: 8.7.8.7.

Suggested Tunes: LOVE DIVINE (Stainer) and BENG-LI

If you have paced your way through woodland, brushing leaves with your feet, watching the oranges, reds and golds scatter in a shower of colour, you will know what I mean by awe! We needn't look out beyond the earth for this vision of creation. We can experience the same sense of wonder on any walk, especially in the autumn, the fall.

The changing shades of the leaves, which can be explained scientifically as the necessary chemical changes enabling trees to divest themselves of waste, bring a glory to the forest canopy, and to the ground on which we walk. I see this beauty in Cheshire where I live, or outside the college where I work in Manchester, or in memory in the colours of North Carolina. Creation can sing to me of God, though I have to look through the eyes of faith to see in this way.

5   The sound of history humming

The sound of history humming,
as light and matter form,
as galaxies are clustered
within a cosmic storm;
philosophers imagine
while science gathers facts,
we reach for understanding,
yet what we know contracts.

We delve beyond the present
through interstellar gas;
we fathom, seek to measure,
a sub-atomic mass.
The God that we conceive of,
a thief within the night,
we cannot gauge this treasure
beyond the scale of light.

As yet the mystery blinds us,
confined by birth and death,
but human exploration
will not discard the quest;
as yet we live in tension:
the only earth we know
is where all skill and science
must help our love to grow.

© Copyright 2006 Stainer & Bell Ltd

Metre: 7.6.7.6.D.

Suggested Tune: VICTORY PARADE

Since writing 'The God of cosmic question' ('Blinded by the Dazzle', Stainer & Bell, 1997) I have explored, through hymns and poetry, the ways in which people, with different skills and learning, have tried to make sense of the cosmos and the world which is our home. This text was written after hearing BBC Radio 4 'Start the Week' contributors speaking of the extremely low frequency hum of black holes. 'The Only Earth We Know' is the title of a collection of hymns by Fred Kaan that has been a great source of inspiration and encouragement to me (Stainer & Bell/Hope Publishing Company, 1999).

VICTORY PARADE

Ian Sharp (1943–)

The sound of his-tory hum-ming, as light and mat-ter form, as ga-la-xies are clus-tered with-in a cos-mic storm; phi--lo-so-phers i-ma-gine while sci-ence ga-thers facts, we reach for un-der-stand-ing, yet what we know con-tracts.

simile

O River-Mother, spirit of creation,
flowing so freely since the dawn of time,
source of all life and onward propagation,
summer's bright warmth and winter's frozen rime.

Once from a riven altar, out through history,
your source of life flowed on to all the earth;
then cosmic letters formed the timeless story,
charged with your passion, grace and love and worth.

Now at the point in time of our existence,
through faith and science we discern our place.
We understand your gentle, calm persistence,
folding around us with your love and grace.

O River-Mother, flowing to the future,
on past the present that we see and feel,
take us, flow with us, kindly love and nurture
virtues that make your presence strong and real.

Metre: 11.10.11.10.

Suggested Tune: O PERFECT LOVE

As my faith has developed I have found the use of feminine images for God particularly helpful. There is nothing radical in this in the twenty-first century. It is impossible to envisage the nature of God aside from the use of metaphor and human allusion, and if we restrict ourselves to male imagery, our ability to speak of God is greatly impoverished. The idea of God mothering creation into being is helpful in balancing the more aggressive masculine images to which we have grown accustomed over centuries. I was watching a film entitled 'The Nun's Story'. I caught in my mind a pun on the appellation 'Reverend Mother'. That began this text, which in no way relates to the film.

The silent stars, the turning globe,
the rivers rushing to the sea;
the certain rising of the sun,
all witness to God's sovereignty;
yet human values shift and drift.
God's wisdom is the greater gift.

Our human toil is wearisome,
while those who die are lost to mind.
Our great endeavours turn to dust,
there's nothing new for us to find.
We chase for rainbows through the rain
and own a deeper loss than gain.

Then what remains for us to do,
what satisfying task or scheme
will fill this endless stream of days,
will help us sound a greater theme?
God give us wisdom, knowledge, joy.
Plant hope that nothing can destroy.

Metre: 8.8.8.8.8 8.

Suggested Tune: OLD 112TH

If our faith is founded on awe and wonder, it becomes difficult to grasp that a loving, all-powerful God has anything to do with the world at all when life goes bad. We are forced to ask awkward questions.

One of the counters to doubt is a profound understanding that, however contradictory it may seem, we are all important to God and that we matter. We are unique and valued children of God. This understanding is rooted in the Bible and set down in narrative and story. Much of this is metaphorical, pointing to an understanding of a people chosen by and precious to God. A whole body of literature in the Bible relates to Wisdom, including Ecclesiastes, which fascinates me. The words above should echo something of the understanding that seeking wisdom can be vain and empty (Ecclesiastes 3:19). Yet wisdom is a gift of God. I understand this. My life has oscillated between an academic thirst for knowledge and a longing for simplicity.

8 With words as sharp as flint

ALLERTON

Ian Sharp (1943–)

With words as sharp as flint, yet e – le – gant – ly said,_____ the
pro-phets spoke the word of God, their_ theme would grow and spread.

With words as sharp as flint,
yet elegantly said,
the prophets spoke the word of God,
their theme would grow and spread.

Here is the choice God gives,
as sharp as any knife,
the choice between your life and death –
choose now, choose right, choose life.

Surrender all to God,
give all you have to give,
then with your neighbour, in God's grace,
come sing, come dance, come live!

Words © Copyright 2006 and Music © Copyright 1988 Stainer & Bell Ltd

Metre: SM

Suggested Tune: ALLERTON

As the theology of the people of Israel grew and evolved, they lived human lives that informed their understanding of God. Contextual theology is nothing new! From slavery in Egypt they moved through the harsh, yet liberating, experience of the Exodus. On the brink of the Promised Land, Moses died. Under Joshua's leadership, the story says, the people moved on and settled into the relative comfort of Canaan. And, like us, the people became complacent. We cry out to God in words that are true prayer, when our needs are greatest. When life is easy, we so easily forget. Prophets then and now remind us of how we ought to be living our lives.

Covenant relationship with God

9   Here before the mountains' grandeur

Here before the mountains' grandeur,
Moses waited, nature hushed;
in the stillness and the beauty,
set apart, no longer rushed.
Here he knelt in awe and wonder,
here in glory, God entrusts.

Once within a towering temple,
filled with smoke, devoid of light,
such a sense of captivation
met Isaiah in the night;
but that meeting made him humble,
then God raised him to the height.

Now wherever God's own presence
breaks into our common ground,
on the mountain, in the temple,
loudly, or without a sound,
there the vision that God offers
challenges all we have found.

Here a different way is offered,
now a fresh resolve is framed,
as the servants of the servant
find that even they are named;
and the call of God is echoed
as each new-found life is claimed.

Metre: 8.7.8.7.8.7.

Suggested Tune: PICARDY

Time and again through my life there have been occasions when I have been drawn back to God. My perception of the nature of that God has varied over the years. Sometimes I have wondered whether this idea of God was created in my imagination. At other times, the sense of it has been intensely real and personal. Sometimes God has spoken with a still small voice inside my head, at others I have been impelled to action. This God has offered comfort, affirmation, reassurance. Often God has spoken through people. Life has offered a series of windows into God. For the people of Israel, history was punctuated by experiences of the presence of God. The nation was led, and individuals felt God guiding them.

Rejoice, for things are as they are;
don't flee as clouds that flow and drift
on wings of wind that shift and change;
God's love will comfort, calm and lift.

For God is your celestial shield,
no cosmic power, nor human scheme
will separate you from that love
no matter how your terrors teem.

Your going out, your coming in
are safe, whatever, come what may.
You know the reason to rejoice,
so sing God's praise by night, by day.

Metre: LM

Suggested Tune: DUNEDIN

The psalmists, and later the New Testament writers, reflected on their recurrent encounters with God. There was a developing sense of God's providence and presence, which enabled them to feel increasingly secure. It was not that bad things stopped happening, or that injustices could not be challenged. In spite of these inevitabilities, through faith they felt secure in God's love.

This hymn, inspired by Psalm 121 and Romans 8: 38–39, is an affirmation of this abiding care of God.

11 The perfect law we fail to keep

The perfect law we fail to keep,
lies damaged, useless, broken;
but in our hearts God whispers love
and peace is gently spoken.

A growing faith can grasp the fact,
God's love is sure, unbending;
and through the flaws and faults of life,
grace mends, is never ending.

A covenant is built around
God's steadfast loving kindness;
and though we strain the trust of friends,
God sees beyond our blindness.

This covenant in which we live
is ours, its love enfolding;
and nothing now in all the world
can wrench us from God's holding.

Metre: 8.7.8.7.

Suggested Tune: ST COLUMBA (Anonymous Irish)

Amongst the Israelites, the idea began to develop that God was in a covenant relationship (a concept derived from a legally binding agreement between two parties) in which the people agreed to do God's will while God agreed to care for them. That was fine till God's commands were broken. The prophet Hosea made it clear that even then God did not abandon them. The theology of the covenant relationship was evolving. Some people have tried to develop a theology in which God changes in response to creation. Even if God does not change, good theology is always dynamic. The most developed expression of the covenant is found in Jeremiah 31:31–33, where God is depicted as saying 'I will put my law within them, and I will write it on their hearts; and I will be their God, and they shall be my people' (NRSV).

12 You are the rainbow's colours

You are the rainbow's colours,
the thundering sighs of love,
the shakers of foundations,
the seething clouds above.
You are God's chosen people,
from exile you are freed,
your common consecration
means liberty indeed.

A hope for every nation,
you come to bring God's peace,
the reconciliation,
the prisoner's release.
This is your sole vocation,
the reason for your birth,
to offer hope through loving,
to bring God's peace on earth.

Metre: 7.6.7.6.D.

Suggested Tune: PASSION CHORALE

Another part of Old Testament theology, which was intrinsically linked with the concept of covenant, was the idea of God's people being a chosen people. They were special. That was not a matter for pride. It had consequences. Firstly, if God loved them in this particular way, they had a responsibility to God. Secondly, they were obliged to work out their relationship with other people. A theology began to develop which looked towards the incorporation of other nations under the banner of God's love. Foreigners were of value. Thirdly came a self-perception that, if they were God's people, they ought to be representative of God to others. To be chosen brought with it not only privilege, but also responsibility.

This hymn gives expression to the sense that all God's people can experience the wonder of chosenness, allied to the consequent responsibility for others that this entails.

When justice is impossible,
beyond our human scope;
when doubt and darkness celebrate
and we no longer cope,
give us, O God, the words to sing,
and faith to trust the end you bring.

From thundercloud, through wind and fire,
you act to bring release.
From bonds that we have forged ourselves
you come to bring us peace;
so give us, God, the words to sing,
and strength to trust the end you bring.

From our distress we call to you,
but yet we fear your hand,
for where we fail you will prevail
but will we live to stand?
O give us God, the words to sing,
whatever end you need to bring.

Our mouths are open with the song,
we're singing for our lives,
bring courage, give us strength, O God,
while human hope survives.
May alleluias fill that song
in spite of all our human wrong.

© Copyright 2006 Stainer & Bell Ltd

Metre: 8.6.8.6.8 8.

Suggested Tune: AUCH JETZT MACHT GOTT

Rightly or wrongly we have the greatest expectations of those with whom we are in close relationship. When they let us down we are hurt out of all proportion. God's people, having developed a theology of chosenness, felt that it was quite appropriate to complain if, from their perspective, God let them down. After all, this God had said, 'I will be their God, and they shall be my people' (Jeremiah 31:33, NRSV). Lament had been born. At least one third of all the psalms are psalms of lament.

The ups and downs of my life have caused me to shout at God from time to time. The psalms are witness to the fact that God can cope with that side of our humanness as well as the 'good' bits of us. Even Jesus lamented on the cross, 'My God, my God, why have you forsaken me?' This text, inspired by Psalm 81, was written at the Lake Junaluska conference and retreat centre in North Carolina after hearing a sermon delivered by Heather Murray Elkins at the Academy of Global Song run by the United Methodist Church Board of Global Ministries.

Such bright green leaves, the auburn fall,
stark trees in winter snow:
a sign of God's perpetual love
as seasons come and go.

The turning planets, misty skies,
the birthing of a star,
the wonders of this universe
we follow from afar.

All nature's light gives pause for thought;
but we should sense this fact,
that God is God of good and ill,
a God of source and act.

The good of God is clear to see,
the evidence is strong,
but can distort our point of view –
what do we make of wrong?

What of the earthquake, wind and fire,
not just the still, small voice?
What of the twister's wild lament
or cancer's random choice?

We must be honest to the view
that nature can display,
God is the God of light and joy,
of carnage and decay.

Metre: CM

Suggested Tune: ST AGNES (Dykes)

Being able to lament is just one part of the story. Lament speaks of honesty, but hymns that reflect on the goodness of God using nature as evidence can be problematic, can appear to be dishonest. Nature is red in tooth and claw. We must be honest about that too, and what it says about God.

15 Fortunes fail while hope is shattered

Fortunes fail while hope is shattered,
nations fall and friendships die.
Who is there to hear our calling,
answer our eternal why?

Language strains to give expression
to the anguish wrapped inside;
anguish at our dislocation,
lacking space in which to hide.

God, where is your promised presence?
Where is your dynamic art,
holding us within your compass,
helping us to play our part?

Metre: 8.7.8.7.

Suggested Tunes: ST CATHERINE (Jones) and GALILEE (Jude)

If we look at things that happen in our lives, then even talk of the constancy of God can sometimes seem to run counter to our experience.

Here they hung their harps:
they could not sing.
The land was new, the language strange,
they could not sing.

Zion was their home,
they'd not forget,
a place of joy, a place of rest,
they'd not forget.

Exiled from that home,
so filled with hate,
they wished their captors slain and dead,
so filled with hate.

God is still their God
so they lament.
But still their God cannot be found,
so they lament.

God is still our God,
and we lament,
and yet frustration fuels our fear.
Yes! We lament.

Metre: 5.4.8.4.

Suggested Tune: WE LAMENT

The depth of despair and anger to which the people of Israel sank was such that they cried out for the people who had wronged them to suffer too.

> *O daughter Babylon, you devastator! Happy shall they be who pay you back what you have done to us!*
> *Happy shall they be who take your little ones and dash them against the rock!*
> *(Psalm 137:8–9, NRSV)*

Marlene Phillips (1933–)

Unison

Here they hung their harps: they could not _ sing.

Harmony

The land was new, the lang-uage strange, they could not

sing,_____ they could not _ sing.

Which allowed lament

17 Beyond the point that we can bear

Beyond the point that we can bear
we cry, O God, to you.
We need your love, your strength, your care –
revisit, God, renew.

An exiled people, trodden down,
bereft, devoid of hope,
we find our hearts dulled by despair,
till we can scarcely cope.

We would not choose to live this way,
it seems your love has gone.
Return to grasp our hands, O God,
return, and lead us on.

Metre: CM

Suggested Tune: GRÄFENBERG (NUN DANKET ALL)

My own experience has challenged my faith, caused me to think, caused me to doubt. Engineers sometimes speak of destructive testing. Life has felt like that, testing me almost to destruction. But I have emerged with a different, stronger faith.

The people of Israel were conquered, taken into exile. Faith and hope seemed dead. They cried out to God, as can we when things seem unbearable.

How long, O Lord, how long
must carnage blight our age?
How long before all humankind
let love disarm their rage?

The streets still run with blood
as dust distils the light;
while buildings clouded by the pall
of smoke are hid from sight.

Our children huddle, dead,
the world seems blind to wrong;
when will your people heed your word?
How long, O Lord, how long?

Metre: SM

Suggested Tunes: TRENTHAM and NARENZA

After a week in which suicide and car bombings dominated the headlines I needed to reflect, and this hymn was the result. When I look at events like these, when I see the carnage of war, I want to cry out to God, to question God, to charge God for not doing anything. I want to ask where God has gone. There is still a place for lament in our world.

LAMENTATION   *Ian Sharp (1943–)*

Si - lenc-ing   the   sing - er   will   nev - er   kill   the   song;   a -

-no-ther voice picks up   the   strain   and   o - thers sing a - long.

Optional descant for verse 4, or sing 'ah'

God will   nev - er   leave____   us;   God will   nev - er   leave____   us.

Silencing the singer
will never kill the song;
another voice picks up the strain
and others sing along.

Out of grief and anguish
another rhyme is bled;
another rhythm beats in time,
eternal tears are shed.

People sing in sorrow,
through anger and through tears,
the ringing song of human grief
will echo down the years.

God will never leave us
despite the death knell's ring.
A hoarse lament is heard again,
God's people always sing.

Metre: 6.6.8.6.

Suggested Tune: LAMENTATION

It is easy to feel despair when confronted by inhumanity, yet the human spirit is strong and, in spite of everything, faith sings out that God is in our anguish and never leaves us. The song goes on. These words were written at Lake Junaluska (see page 15) after hearing a sermon delivered by Heather Murray Elkins at the Academy of Global Song run by the United Methodist Church Board of Global Ministries.

20 When we are sidelined and taken for granted

When we are sidelined and taken for granted,
used and abused and when none seems to care;
God never leave us, forsake us, forget us,
give us the faith that, though suffering, can dare.

When we are paralysed, guilty and grieving,
shunned by our friends, hurt, despised and in pain;
hold us and lift us, renew and refresh us,
give us new life that we might live again.

When we're abandoned, alone and deserted,
drowned in the torrent, or lost in life's stream;
temper this torment and shield from destruction,
prove to us, God, that your love's not a dream.

Metre: 11.10.11.10.

Suggested Tune: LIEBSTER IMMANUEL

The hymn 'What a friend we have in Jesus' contains the phrase 'Do thy friends despise, forsake thee?'. The words of that hymn are reassuring. In similar circumstances the psalmist would have lamented and cried out to God for help. Our own human experience is more likely to begin in lament than in assurance unless our faith is very firm or we are denying much that is going on around us. This hymn cries out to God for a sign that the love of which we've heard is not just a dream.

21   We have sung because we had to

We have sung because we had to,
singing to survive;
out of hardship, bondage, danger,
singing to survive.

We are singing to the Godhead,
singing to survive;
praise and thanks and celebration,
singing to survive.

Join the song, yes, join your neighbour,
singing to survive.
Hand in hand let's walk together,
singing to survive.

On beyond this world, this lifetime,
singing to survive.
Singing with the saints before us,
singing to survive.

Metre: 8.5.8.5.

Suggested Tune: GOD, YOU HOLD ME

*Singing with others can have a profound effect on us. Think of people singing 'We shall overcome'
in the face of injustice or hostility. Imagine black slaves encouraging each other. Singing can bind
the oppressed together. This hymn comes out of the belief that singing can strengthen our will to
survive in the face of injustice, and was written after hearing George Mulrain, President of the
Methodist Church in the Caribbean and Americas, speaking of Caribbean song.*

And still allows lament

GOD, YOU HOLD ME

George F. Bexon (1958–)

We have sung be - cause we had to, sing-ing to sur-

-vive; out of hard - ship, bon - dage, dan - ger,

sing-ing to sur - vive. -vive.

And still allows lament

22　In every face we see the pain

In every face we see the pain
of grief and human loss;
the hell we cannot understand,
we cannot count the cost.
In each disaster we recount
earth's shifting, changing ways.
Creation brings its agony,
a challenge to our praise.

And was God midwife at the birth
confounding our belief?
Or is our God outside the frame,
removed from human grief?
For ages we have tried and failed
to understand this flaw:
that God should let such evil rise,
while mixing love and awe.

If God is here, where bodies break,
where life seems so much dross,
where are the mercy, grace and love,
the gift of crib and cross?
We plead for love, we long for grace,
to help us, where they fell,
to grasp the reason for this pain,
this cavalcade of hell.

Then give us strength to rise again,
enlivened by your hope,
and for the present show your love
and give us grace to cope.
God, come and join your people in
the centre of their loss.
If you are real then show yourself
upon this present cross.

Metre: CMD

Suggested Tune: KINGSFOLD

Natural disasters raise difficult questions and we cry out for answers. This hymn was written in response to the tsunami which took place on 26 December 2004.

As wandering Arameans
we make each land our home,
we take our memories with us,
whichever way we roam.
Experience is gathered,
new hope and faith are found;
and all the earth is holy,
each place is holy ground.

Our God is walking with us
through every place and time.
This friend will never leave us
for love remains the sign:
as wandering Arameans,
we'll make the world our home;
we'll take our memories with us,
whichever way we roam.

Metre: 7.6.7.6.D.

Suggested Tunes: PENLAN and MERLE'S TUNE

Trying to keep close to God is never easy. There have been times when I've wanted evidence for God just 'being there'. I go to a particular location that 'feels good'. In this place it is easy to sense the presence of God. But I move on. What then? The early story of Israel is of a wandering people, seemingly rootless, but always looking towards a place where they might settle. And through all this, God is constant and they build memories of what has happened to reassure themselves, to which they return when assailed by doubt. And, for me, when faith is small, I go back to events, to places, to memories, to remind me that God is still there in spite of all that is going on around me.

These words were written after hearing the composer Carlton Young speaking about the memories that communities carry and nurture.

As the watchmen wait for morning,
so we wait, and yearn for God;
as disciples followed Jesus,
we seek solace where he trod.

Clouds have covered what we hope for
and we stumble in the dark,
faith is chilled and love is frozen,
everything is bare and stark.

Yet we sense that somewhere, hidden
in the shadows, out of sight,
God remains and will awaken
dormant grace that kindles light.

Darkness leaves, uncomprehending;
we will never be bereft.
Light is dawning, Christ is coming,
we will follow in love's quest.

Metre: 8.7.8.7.

Suggested Tunes: WYCHBOLD and RATHBUN

Our pilgrimage continues. We wait for God. We long for God. Sometimes we look for God. We mirror again the age-old human longing to make sense of our lives. One of my wife's favourite passages is from the first chapter of John, the verse that speaks of the light coming into the world and the darkness never overcoming it. An old translation speaks of the darkness not comprehending the light. I like that image. It is echoed in the last verse of this text. It also reflects my own sense of pilgrimage, which is so often that of waiting, stumbling and wondering, with just occasional signals that the light of God's love has not and never will be extinguished.

The singing of the angels
beyond the smoke and veil:
a temple shakes like thunder,
God's spirit will prevail.

Isaiah feels forgiveness,
and then the heavenly call,
that summons out of nowhere
to go, to give his all.

We witness his conversion
before the Godhead's throne;
and we would mark his footsteps
and, in them, place our own.

Metre: 7.6.7.6.

Suggested Tunes: FORGIVENESS (Gesius) and CHRISTUS DER IST MEIN LEBEN

I have always been amazed when I've had a sense of the closeness of God and then discovered how it mirrors that of other people. Sometimes there is a need to draw away the veil of centuries or the obscurity brought about by language and culture. There is a rich tradition of sensing God's presence which runs through history from Moses, through the prophets and down through the Christian mystics, and is echoed in other traditions and faiths. To stand in that line is to be aware of immense privilege and awe, to be 'lost in wonder, love and praise' as Charles Wesley put it. This hymn reflects on that heritage as it looks back to the conversion of Isaiah.

JERUSALEM   J. B. Dykes (1823–76)

Sheer si - lence greets E - li - jah, be - yond_the wind_ and_ fire;   the

whis - per_ of   a   heaven-ly__ voice, no__ sing - ing   by   a   choir.

Sheer silence greets Elijah,
beyond the wind and fire;
the whisper of a heavenly voice,
no singing by a choir.

It stunned him to submission,
still cowering in that cleft,
compelled by passion, hid from light,
he'd only one way left.

The power that seized his substance
now spoke to charge his heart,
confronting what had brought retreat,
revealing map and chart.

The present is discarded,
the past is far behind;
the future needs his gift and skill,
his courage and his mind.

And so, back to the valley,
where God is always near,
the spirit guides the prophet's feet,
to all that fired his fear.

Metre: 7.6.8.6.

Suggested Tune: JERUSALEM (Dykes)

With not a little fear Elijah ran from people, from God, from responsibility (1 Kings 19:9–18), but out in the wilderness he heard God speaking in a whisper.

27   Subtle, enigmatic God

LOVING CUP   *Andrew Pratt (1948–)*

Subtle, enigmatic God:
quieter than our prayer;
hidden when we seek you most,
veiled, yet always there.

Hidden in each branch and root,
heard as babies cry,
carried on a dying breath,
deeper than a sigh.

Closer to us than ourselves,
yet still out of sight;
present in the deepest gloom,
and the blinding light.

Spirit, open up our eyes,
touch each sense with grace,
that in those that share this earth
we'll discern your face.

Metre: 7.5.7.5.

Suggested Tune: LOVING CUP

The editorial of the 'Epworth Review', April 2004, spoke of God as hidden yet present all around, especially in those of other faiths. I am sure that, while the revelation of God to each faith is unique, God can be discerned in and out of the trappings of those faiths. If the incarnation means anything, then we see God, and Christ, in others. And this is another step on the journey of the mystic. God is not always remote, not always in the mountains or on the seashore – though our awareness may be heightened there – but in the people who throng around us, who need our care and offer that care to us.

With clouded minds we search and try to fathom
the nature of a God we cannot see;
and in the end we bow before the mystery:
this love that binds can really set us free.

When using every source at our disposal,
each heart, each dance and every prophet's dream,
the power of intellect, the things we measure,
we only catch a glimpse of love's great scheme.

We feel our way, we reach into the future,
aware that God was with us in the past;
we seek a clear perspective for the present,
assured that love, unlimited, will last.

Metre: 11.10.11.10.

Suggested Tune: INTERCESSOR

My scientific training has caused me to approach the examination of my faith with the same curiosity and rigour. I delight in nature. But none of this provided the answers that I sought. Faith should not be beyond intellectual critique, but it is sometimes strangely resistant to it. We try to understand God, but this God is, by definition, beyond understanding.

The suck of surf through shingle,
the hush of turning tide,
the rolling, rhythmic thunder:
that chaos God would ride.
Across the foaming waters
a spirit soared and spilled
until the coarse confusion
was challenged, held and stilled.

Leviathan would play there,
an ark was tossed and turned,
disciples lost their sea-legs
as Galilee was churned.
The water mirrored evil,
a symbol of the hell
that drowned the hopes and wishes
of those caught in its swell.

A metaphor for anguish,
commotion without God,
a place where love seemed vanquished,
where hatred's footsteps trod.
But walking on that water
and stilling waves of rage,
where maddened swine had floundered
God's love had come of age.

Metre: 7.6.7.6.D.

Suggested Tunes: CHARTRES and AURELIA

I was brought up by the sea, and its images become more evocative the older I get. The sea was seen as dangerous and even evil by the writers of the Bible. God could control the waters and bring order out of the seeming chaos, and when Jesus walked on water the association with God was clear. From the opposite perspective, Jesus cured a man by sending the spirits possessing him into a herd of pigs that plunged over the cliff into the Sea of Galilee – symbolically back to the hell from which they had come.

When the American composer Carson Cooman asked for a text with images of the sea from the Bible, I welcomed the challenge.

I will not let you go without a blessing,
all night beside the brook we toss and turn;
a nameless one you struggle, not confessing
from where you came, or where you will return.

My limping life is evidence of meeting,
of wrestling with God from dusk till dawn,
within this place, a place of stuttered greeting,
where riddles cloud the questions that we spawn.

And yet in spite of doubt, while disbelieving,
you leave sufficient pause for me to think
that this frail frame can be the ground conceiving
new life, new birth, returning from the brink.

Renamed, reclaimed, your servant, I stand waiting
to hear the new commission for my days;
I bow my head in prayer anticipating
the words to send me on in ceaseless praise.

Metre: 11.10.11.10.

Suggested Tune: ANSTRUTHER

Part of the mythology of the Bible concerns the meeting of people directly with God. Whether this is metaphor or reality it has mirrored for me some of my own experience. The struggle of coming to faith, then coming to terms with faith, then making decisions informed by faith is familiar. The Bible tells the story of Jacob wrestling with a stranger at the Jabbok Brook, and his being renamed Israel. This hymn is suitable for adult baptism, confirmation or reaffirmation of commitment.

ANSTRUTHER

Peter Cutts (1937–)

I will not let__ you go with - out a bles - sing,
all night be - side__ the brook we toss and turn;
a name - less one__ you strug - gle, not__ con - fes - sing
from where you came,_ or where_ you will re - turn.

A nation buried in the dust,
the death of life, the end of trust,
the desert wind, the caustic sun,
oppression's work was finished, done.

A prophet watched this silent scene,
and thought of all that might have been;
a vision formed within his mind,
the God he knew was gracious, kind.

The burning wind, God's vital breath,
would blow across this place of death,
the people come to life again,
the desert feel the touch of rain.

And so Ezekiel offered hope,
a means of grace, a way to cope;
the smouldering wick would flash to flame,
the nation rise to life again.

The proof of all he had to say
was tested on another day;
as Cyrus came to set them free,
the people gained their liberty.

Metre: LM

Suggested Tunes: EISENACH and TALLIS'S CANON

At those times when God seems far off we may feel abandoned. For individuals, even for nations, these times can be profound turning points, times of growth and learning about the nature of God. The abandonment of the people of Israel, taken into exile in Babylon, can mirror our own times of dryness and emptiness. Ezekiel provided a stunning vision of a valley filled with dry bones coming to life, saying to the people they were not alone and God would bring them back. Isaiah tells how Cyrus became God's instrument, setting them free and allowing them to return home. The most unusual people can be the source of our salvation.

Deep in darkness we begin,
dark outside and deep within.
Now ignite a single flame,
shadows form, let light remain.

As they gleaned the word of life,
narrative of love and strife,
people through each age have known
yet more light: God's glory shown.

John the Baptist spoke out loud,
challenged that discordant crowd,
called each one toward the light,
see it growing, gleaming bright.

Mary wondered at her lot,
blessed? Or cursed? Or loved? Or not?
Angels came and glory shone.
Feel the love, let light shine on.

Look! a star is shining there.
See the stable stark and bare.
Christmas dawns, all darkness gone!
Christ has come, the light shines on!

Metre: 7 7.7 7.

Suggested Tunes: LAUDS (Wilson) and ORIENTIS PARTIBUS

As I came to faith it was natural for me, as a scientist, to test everything. I then became less sceptical, more evangelical in the popular sense of the word. Life, however, made me profoundly sceptical again. But I retained an overriding sense of the importance of Jesus. Metaphysical things seemed much less tangible. What could we make of Jesus if he were only human? We begin in darkness with a candle-lighting hymn for the Sundays of Advent.

In the heat of summer sunshine,
source of energy on earth,
here the dayspring, daylight dawning,
shining light has human birth.

Mary, mother, lies exhausted,
bloodied baby gasps for breath;
now creation's expectation
finds fruition: God in flesh.

Light for here and every nation,
in the brightest of our days,
source of all incarnate with us,
cooled, contained, that cosmic blaze.

Here we greet a revolution,
earth is turning from the night,
son of David, child of Mary
framed in time, eternal light.

Metre: 8.7.8.7.

Suggested Tune: WYCHBOLD

The time of Advent is a time of moving from emptiness to revelation and from darkness to light, but in Australia everything is turned upside down. The seasons feel all wrong. Rex Hunt, a theologian, liturgist, social ecologist and minister of the Uniting Church in Australia, asked for a Christmas hymn that understood this. Trying to write it I was forced back to the bare reality of the first night in that stable and the real theological significance of the event.

Mid silence and stillness, imagine the sight,
great flashes of brilliance cascade through the night,
all heaven is ringing to waken the earth,
as angels are singing and God comes to birth.

A sonorous cadence, then sensitive chords,
enable our worship, creation applauds.
Transcending all limits, through gifts they are given,
musicians are bringing us glimpses of heaven.

In music God gives, through each genre and style,
a solace when weeping, new joy to a smile;
we celebrate colour, each gift and each skill,
applying our art to the goal of God's will.

We join with the angels in praising our God;
we follow the saints on the paths that they trod.
Sing holy, sing highly, come raise up your voice:
O sing Alleluia! Yes! Praise and rejoice!

Metre: 11 11.11 11.

Suggested Tune: AWAY IN A MANGER

Praise becomes attractive even for the sceptic! As we move towards Christmas, praise is natural. Janice McNair, Director of Music at the First-Centenary United Methodist Church, Chattanooga, Tennessee, commissioned this hymn to mark the retirement of the church's organist, Dr Walker Breland.

The crib and the stable are waiting,
the shepherds have gathered around;
the Magi have noticed a new shining star,
the child that they sought has been found.

Yet now in the streets of that city
the talk is of carnage and fear,
the peace of the saviour seems distant, unreal,
the thunder of war yet too near.

And now as we meet to remember,
as Christmas has come round again,
the tinsel, the tree, and the presents soon pass,
through action God's love can remain.

Metre: 9.8.11.8.

Suggested Tune: LITHE SPIRIT

Arriving at Christmas we are confronted by some of the most challenging credal statements of the church. What do we make of the virgin birth? How do we react to the idea of Jesus as the Son of God? Some Biblical critics tell us that the idea of a virgin giving birth was based on a mistranslation of the Old Testament. That doesn't take away the tradition of the church in which so many of us have been nurtured, reinforced by our hymns, carols and Christmas festivities. We'll return to the questions; but first we need to reclaim the reality of a wretched birth, and then make something of that birth for people today. This carol was written in 2004 for the 100th anniversary carol service of my old school, Torquay Grammar School for Boys.

The crib and the sta - ble are wait - ing,_____ the
shep-herds have gath-ered a - round;_____ the Ma - gi have no-ticed a
new shi-ning star, the child that they sought has been found._____

We see the birth of Jesus

36 God is born among us: earth receives the Christ child

God is born among us: earth receives the Christ child,
all the night awakens, light dispels the darkness.
Joyful angels raise an anthem singing praises to the heavens:
gloria, gloria, gloria, in excelsis Deo!
Joyful angels raise an anthem singing praises to the heavens:
gloria, gloria, gloria, in excelsis Deo!

In the fields the shepherds heard the angel chorus:
'Leave your sheep, go quickly, Bethlehem is calling!'
There the Lord had come among us; God redeeming all creation:
gloria, gloria, gloria, in excelsis Deo!
There the Lord had come among us; God redeeming all creation:
gloria, gloria, gloria, in excelsis Deo!

All the hosts of heaven, all the heavenly powers,
tell the story clearly, but we are confounded.
This transcends our understanding, here in awe we gaze in wonder:
gloria, gloria, gloria, in excelsis Deo!
This transcends our understanding, here in awe we gaze in wonder:
gloria, gloria, gloria, in excelsis Deo!

Metre: 12.12.16.15.16.15.

Suggested Tune: GDY SIE CHRYSTUS RODZI

In translation we follow what others have written. I was introduced to this text, 'Gdy się Chrystus rodzi' by Keith Trencher, who travels widely in Eastern Europe working for reconciliation. I was captivated by the tune and wanted to make the Polish words accessible to my congregation in Orrell Church Street Methodist Church, in the Orrell and Lamberhead Green Circuit. (From the Polish of Por. Mioduszewski, Pastorałki 1843)

Traditional Polish
Arranged Ian Sharp (1943–)

Brightly

God is born a -
all the night a -

-mong us: earth re-ceives the Christ child,
-wa - kens, light dis-pels the dark - ness.

Optional descant (2nd time only)
glo - ri - a,

Joy-ful an-gels raise an an-them

glo - ri - a, glo - ri-a, glo - ri-a, glo - ri-a,

sing-ing-prai-ses to the hea-vens: glo - ri-a, glo - ri-a, glo - ri-a,

1
in ex-cel-sis

2
De - o, De - o!

in ex - cel - sis De - o! De - o!

Arrangement © Copyright 2006 Stainer & Bell Ltd

We see the birth of Jesus

43

37   At the census in the city

At the census in the city,
at the crossing place of life,
where the homeless and abandoned
share the scars of human strife;
mid the rubble and the ruins
shedding God's prophetic light,
see, a star is softly shining
through the horror of the night.

In the cross of shafting shadows
see a mother and her child,
see the wetness of his features,
freshly born, so not yet filed.
In a world of cold statistics,
yet another mouth to feed,
for the parents' love holds tension
with a calling, crying need.

So from Bethlehem in history
to this present place and time,
God has entered human anguish,
sung in tune to human rhyme;
yes, the baby that we welcome,
yes, the Christ of Palestine,
are as one, we seal remembrance
in a feast of bread and wine.

For the ruin of the manger,
this prefiguring of the cross,
offers Christ as our relation
in our chaos and our loss,
puts the Christ into the present,
places God in human hands,
tests our loving and our living
here in this and every land.

Metre: 8.7.8.7.D.

Suggested Tunes: BETHANY (Smart) and ABBOT'S LEIGH

Jenny Spouge, a colleague in the Methodist ministry, had written: 'It struck me that there might be something for a hymn writer such as you when the place of Christ's birth is currently rather in need of redemption. Any chance that might fuel the creative juices?' As the text evolved it became not just a Christmas hymn but one linked to Easter and suitable for communion. It was published in 'Worship Live' and in the 'Methodist Recorder' at Christmas 2003.

We used to think of snow and ice,
of children making merry;
of trees bedecked with shining lights,
of holly bright with berry.
But as we celebrate today
the baby in a manger,
remind us how you loved, in life,
both enemy and stranger.

We spend and hoard to comfort us
within the chill of winter.
Remind us of each present pain
you challenge us to enter;
then hand in hand with those in need
and sharing in their coldness,
we might proclaim with louder voice
the gospel in its boldness.

And only when the world is fed
and all oppression ended,
when songs of joy replace the screams
that human war extended,
can we in honesty of heart,
with Mary in her wonder,
reclaim our faith's integrity
as alleluias thunder.

Metre: 8.7.8.7.D.

Suggested Tune: BISHOPGARTH   MI 1597

Written as a Christmas greeting for my wife, Jackie. In this text I continued to explore the tension between the Christmas of tradition and the Christmas of reality.

We see the birth of Jesus

Here in this day's incarnation,
as a child is brought to birth,
God is in this bright creation,
saying 'yes' to human worth.

In each birth, in all our living,
times of joy and sorrow too,
reminiscing or forgiving,
God is making each day new.

Take each moment, live with fervour
every second, day or night,
God is there, a keen observer,
childlike, sharing our delight.

Metre: 8.7.8.7.

Suggested Tunes: ALL FOR JESUS and EMMAUS (Sedio)

My faith has to be worked out against the panorama of experience within which my life is set. As my niece and nephew Emma and Jamie awaited the birth of their child, every moment was charted and cherished, every movement extolled. And I imagine God observing with unfettered delight these expressions of unselfconscious love!

There shone a star at the start of creation,
beaming so brightly through time and through space;
sign of God's presence, divine conflagration,
opening the way for each child of our race.

That star would shine when the prophets were speaking,
shining to show what was false, what was true.
Still that light shines when God's people are seeking
lives that are frail to build up and renew.

Then a new star marked the birthplace of Jesus,
herald of hope at the coming of God.
We hear again, now the story has caught us,
follow the footsteps that shepherds once trod.

This was the star that shone all through that Christmas
leading the Magi to love and to grace;
leading us still, to the God who has sought us,
looking with longing from every child's face.

Metre: 11.10.11.10.

Suggested Tunes: EPIPHANY HYMN and WESLEY (Lowell Mason)

As the seasons change the liturgical calendar offers an opportunity for us to make sense of the events of the gospel story. These words were written for the Toy Service at Bispham Methodist Church in the Orrell and Lamberhead Green Circuit, 14 December 2003.

41   Weird strangers, out of place in Bethlehem

Weird strangers, out of place in Bethlehem,
stargazers who predict and chart and gauge:
what triggered these perceptive, ancient men?
What added their incongruence to this stage?

Flamboyant dress brings colour to this scene,
their clothes of silk, their rich symbolic gifts;
what once had been so rural, rustic, mean,
is royal, regal, as perception shifts.

No ragged child is born amid the herd,
as exiled parents struggle to survive.
Our God is come! The story is absurd:
the ground of all existence is alive!

Metre: 10.10.10.10.

Suggested Tune: JULIUS   MI 1521

Some characters in the Christmas story we accept without question. But what would those kings have looked like in a cowshed? These words for Epiphany were first used at Orrell Methodist Church in the Orrell and Lamberhead Green Circuit of the British Methodist Church.

We see the birth of Jesus

42   The kindness of a God

The kindness of a God
of universal care,
was sounded in Isaiah's day
to all who were aware.

The goodness of that God,
condensed to purest love,
was put into a manger-bed,
but would that be enough?

A window into grace,
divinity distilled,
where shepherds, Magi, celebrate
here all the earth was stilled.

That stillness soon was tried
as Herod worked his ill,
disturbed and threatened by this child
who'd manifest God's will.

And so, through all those years,
while kindness, goodness, strained
to overcome our selfishness,
love, and a cross, remained.

Metre: SM

Suggested Tune: NARENZA   MI 138|

Seeking to make sense of the incarnation I have returned many times to the Christmas narrative. Yet traditional views of incarnation strain my understanding. So here I have explored the idea of Jesus being 'a window into grace', God's goodness 'distilled to purest love' — an image from my scientific background. In the end, for me, pure goodness and love are seen in Jesus, and that is enough. The words were begun on 28 December 2001, Holy Innocents Day.

The birth of a boy-child, the growth of a man:
his mother's enigma; a part of God's plan?
Uncertain, now standing a part of the crowd;
the still of the water foreshadows a shroud.

The death of an old life, the birth of a new,
as values are challenged, past choices askew.
Fierce currents of feeling, encounters of love,
a man by a river, a voice and a dove.

That voice stills the crowd at the slow river's rim:
'My son, my beloved, now listen to him.'
The birth of a boy-child, the growth of a man:
his mother's enigma; a part of God's plan?

Metre: 11 11.11 11.

Suggested Tune: AWAY IN A MANGER

We shroud the truth of the history of our faith in metaphysical images. The truth is often more startling. Life grounded on this earth in the midst of humanity is more helpful than images of angels and metaphysics, which make no sense to twenty-first-century minds. So we watch Jesus come to birth and grow into a man. Let me begin with a hymn on the baptism of Jesus. In 'The Guardian' newspaper there was a review of Julie Orringer's 'How to Breathe Underwater', by Anthony Quinn. A photograph of the author was entitled 'Fierce currents of feeling'. I began writing with these words.

Walk with us God through your creation
as Jesus walked toward a cross.
Face with us every contradiction,
incessant joy and utter loss.

Where are the marks of crucifixion
in hands with which we seek to serve?
How do we handle harsh derision,
or human praise we don't deserve?

Out in the world where you are damaged,
where human lives are ground to dust,
though we are torn, dishevelled, ravaged,
restore our faith, retain our trust.

Go with us on beyond the present,
bearing the scars that life has brought,
on to the future, where you want us,
on in the grace that faith has caught!

Metre: 9.8.9.8.

Suggested Tune: ST CLEMENT

It is real life that we are called to live, but real life that finds its inspiration and reason in Jesus. For Christians he is the one we should emulate, but we rarely do. These words were written in response to the words of the then President and Vice-President of the Methodist Conference, the Rev. Dr Neil Richardson and Mrs Judy Jarvis.

Seeing salvation, a vision of heaven:
doors to God's glory are flung open wide;
here in the face of the hungry or homeless
Jesus is present and hope can reside.

This unexpected, though God-given presence,
stark, cold reality captures the eye;
surely this poverty cannot encompass
Jesus' divinity, prophecy's sigh?

Here, in simplicity, here on the pavement,
under the arches, down rain-sodden roads
Jesus is walking, through saddened eyes staring,
loving the broken and easing their loads.

Metre: 11.10.11.10.

Suggested Tune: LIEBSTER IMMANUEL

I have increasing difficulty in taking on board traditional explanations of the atonement and salvation which derive from metaphysical speculation. I need a faith which is rooted and grounded in the real world of real people in which I live. I am happy for 'sidewalk' to replace 'pavement' where this is more appropriate (verse 3).

Behind a piercing certainty
he hid a smiling face;
his words, profound simplicity
and self-effacing grace.

Perceptive and intuitive,
compassionate, yet strong;
he sensed the depth of human hurt
and challenged what was wrong.

Confronted with hypocrisy,
self-righteousness and cant,
he stood for honesty and truth,
refusing to recant.

It seems this Galilean man
could help us to observe
divinity within the world,
could touch a human nerve.

But this is more than we can bear,
it undermines our pride,
exposes every ruthless plan,
the love we have denied.

'This is the son of God,' we hear
a soldier quietly sigh
as, looking up through tear-stained eyes,
he watches justice die.

Metre: CM

Suggested Tunes: ASCENDIT (German Traditional) and AMAZING GRACE

The more I reach back to the image of Jesus in the gospels the more real he becomes. I would want to call myself 'evangelical' because I take the evangel, the gospel, seriously. To do that I can no longer read the Bible superficially. I need to use all the tools at my disposal to uncover the reality of Jesus, to enable that Jesus to be relevant today. These tools include biblical scholarship and the imaginations of poets and dramatists.

God's learning to be free beneath
the shadow of a waiting cross,
where hammered nails, the silver fee,
sum up immeasurable loss.

Immeasurable loss contends
with grace across the universe,
while love is focused, never ends,
and strains to overcome the curse;

To overcome the curse of death,
this calculated agony,
while hate annihilates his breath,
death's pain and death is all they see.

And death is all they see, this day,
a body dying on a tree.
But dancing now in heaven's way:
Amen! God's learning to be free!

Metre: LM

Suggested Tune: WAREHAM

While Jesus lived with the disciples, he taught them the cruel truth that following him could be harsh and not easy, a lesson we still need to learn.

When we come down from the mountain,
going back to things we know,
give us love and understanding,
there and then your grace may grow.

In each daily situation
keep alive the joy we found,
help us know, in spite of all things,
every day we're heaven-bound.

In each mundane occupation,
in the routine paths of life,
let us share God's peace and healing,
there and then dispelling strife.

As each neighbour shares this blessing,
sown by God within our lives;
we'll know nothing has been wasted,
there and then God's love survives.

Metre: 8.7.8.7.

Suggested Tunes: IN BABILONE and ST OSWALD

From time to time we reach peaks of faith, times of certainty, after which we return to the mundane, ordinary things of life. It's then that the strength of our resolve is tested. We need God with us as much in the mundane as in the spectacular. We need to see Christ in one other, not just in ecstatic spiritual moments. These words were written during the Liverpool Methodist District Synod for Bispham Methodist Church's weekend in Coniston, 2003.

Putting down words, quickening people,
something that songster–pastor did,
loved like a songbird, lived for the singing,
craved for the love God lived.

Shepherd for sheep, far beyond holding,
reaching outside accepted space,
reached for the losers, never forsaking,
offered abnormal grace.

Victim of love, love that he offered,
something that songster–pastor felt;
died for the people, would not deny them,
whether they screamed or knelt.

Pastor and priest, lover of people,
joining that round, that laughing rill,
chorus and cantor, singing together,
shepherds the people still.

Metre: 9.8.10.6.

Suggested Tune: PUTTING DOWN WORDS

The last text in this section is imaginative, folksy. The songster–pastor is the human Jesus.

PUTTING DOWN WORDS

Peter Sharrocks (1940–)

Put-ting down words,   quick-en-ing peo - ple,   some-thing that song-ster—

pas - tor did,   loved like a song-bird,   lived for the sing-ing,   craved for the love God

lived.   still_____   shep-herds the peo - ple   still.

How insignificant we are
beneath the mountains ranged above;
and filled with awe we fall before
the God that we would name as love.

As eagles soar beyond our sight
on thermals rising through the air;
we look into the blinding light
and try to find the Godhead there.

We fall from light, but not from grace,
we live amid life's hurts and harms;
we wonder, wander, never lost,
held by the everlasting arms.

And when we grasp the depths of love,
in Christ our lives are whole, complete;
we gaze in awe, our eyes raised up,
then sense God kneeling at our feet.

Metre: LM

Suggested Tunes: BRESLAU and CANONBURY (Schumann)

For me, some of the most profound and moving experiences have come about as I have reflected on the human nature of Jesus and the way in which his life provides a window into the nature of God. Theologians like Jürgen Moltmann opened a generation's eyes to the vulnerability of God. Liberation theology worked on the premise that theology was made in community by ordinary people as they explored the Bible and made the narrative their own. So in my imagination I look out at, say, a vista of the Austrian Tyrol. Against the mountains as humans we are tiny; the more so if we look beyond to the immensity of the cosmos. Jesus's life and action says that in spite of this we are all of ultimate significance. God is very down-to-earth.

Come with joy to offer worship,
meet your neighbour face to face,
offer her the hand of greeting,
share this fountain of God's grace.
Bring the bread of loving kindness,
channel love to heart and mind,
bringing glory to this meeting,
calm and comforting and kind.

Bring the wine of celebration
to this eucharistic feast;
where all gifts and lives are welcome,
where each person finds release.
Handle mysteries, make them friendly,
join together, offer prayer;
live the meaning of your singing,
seeing Christ in all who share.

Metre: 8.7.8.7.D.

Suggested Tunes: PLEADING SAVIOUR (SALTASH), PROMISE (Sleeth) and ALL FOR JESUS (when sung as four verses)

Sharing a meal is an intimate and a trusting way to relate to other people. It should not surprise us that religious rites have often centred on food. Though we can trace the beginnings of communion to the Last Supper, as either a sabbath or passover meal, I believe that for the early Christians this celebration was an ordinary meal. The disciples 'shared their meals with unaffected joy' (Acts 2:46, NEB). Whenever they ate they would remember Jesus. Not just on special, ritual occasions. If we understand that, then it becomes not some mysterious celebration, some arcane process, which is bound by rules to 'make sure we do it right' and say the necessary words in the correct order. This hymn was written at Lake Junaluska, at the Academy of Global Song run by the United Methodist Church Board of Global Ministries, after I heard Carlton Young quote Erik Routley's words, 'Handle mysteries, make them friendly'. If sung as four verses it can be used to frame communion – verse one followed by The Peace, verse two followed by the offertory of the bread, verse three followed by the offertory of the wine and the Institution, then verse four, after which communion is shared.

We come without pretension,
our pride is put aside,
we make this calm communion
as, standing side by side,
we lose our love of self
and gain eternal wealth.

Such simple gifts of harvest:
you give us bread and wine
and, by the words remembered,
these form a special sign
of love, a greater deep,
of grace for us to keep.

Then, rising from this table,
forgiven, loved and free,
we raise an acclamation
and all the world can see
the love we find in you,
while gaining all things new.

Metre: 7.6.7.6.6 6.

Suggested Tune: KNUZDEN

Communion is an opportunity to share without pretension in divine simplicity. As in death, here at the table we all should be equal.

Marlene Phillips (1933–)

We come with-out pre - ten - sion, our pride is put a - side,＿＿ we

make this calm com - mun - ion as, stand -ing side by side,＿＿ we

lose our love of self＿＿ and gain＿＿＿＿＿ e - ter - nal＿ wealth.

53 All the world is holy

VERITY

Ian Sharp (1943–)

All the world is ho - ly:___ God is in this place,___ re - cog -
- nise the pre - sence hov - ering in___ this space.

All the world is holy:
God is in this place,
recognise the presence
hovering in this space.

Things are frail, they perish,
words will hurt the flesh;
human lives are broken,
people die unblessed.

Love will call us outwards,
love will take us on,
challenging injustice,
always righting wrong.

Handle God with caution,
hesitant you stand.
Sing with joy, for certain,
judgement is at hand.

Metre: 6.5.6.5.

Suggested Tune: VERITY

Scripture warns us against taking communion without discerning the body of Christ. Theologians have all too often interpreted this mystically as relating to the transubstantiation of the bread. A simpler, more profound and, dare I say sensible, explanation is to take that discernment to refer to our sisters, our brothers, those who make up the body of Christ in Paul's understanding of it. If this is accepted, every time we take communion we are confronted with challenge and judgement in relation to the love we have for our neighbour. That seems to me to be far more in keeping with the Jesus who complained about hypocrites straining gnats out of drinking water while letting the hungry starve. These words were written at Lake Junaluska, at the Academy of Global Song run by the United Methodist Church Board of Global Ministries, after I heard Heather Murray Elkins lecturing.

Share the last supper

Such a mystery, bread is taken,
grace is given, love is sown;
here in acts of loving kindness,
simple sharing, faith is grown.

Such amazement, God-forgiven
humble people kneel to pray;
stripped of every self-deception,
this is not an idle play.

Such enlightened self-awareness,
meeting Jesus face to face;
conscious of our need for changing,
need of God's transforming grace.

Such polite commemoration,
goes beyond our self-pretence,
speaks of mutual need and caring,
loving 'in the present tense'.

Metre: 8.7.8.7.

Suggested Tune: ALL FOR JESUS

For some people communion provides a profound, inexplicable experience. One of my students said that sharing communion made her tingle! 'Such a tingle' then became 'Such a mystery'. The phrase 'loving in the present tense' echoes a line in Sydney Carter's song 'Present Tense': 'Give me the good news in the present tense.'

55 'Let them eat bread,' as Jesus said

'Let them eat bread,' as Jesus said.
'Drink wine to bring me to your mind.'
But more important is the love
that shows us true and kind.

Let them greet children in my name,
the ones who have no guile or power;
then welcome sinners, those oppressed,
whose lives are bleak or sour.

Now as we take the broken bread,
we dignify each living soul,
and then the mystery that we share
will make God's people whole.

Metre: 8.8.8.6.

Suggested Tune: MISERICORDIA (Smart)

This text is another attempt to address the theme that we discern Christ's body in communion when we realise that the 'body' is the body of humanity in the world.

'So, good night Judas, on your way,
go out into the night.
You have a task you need to do
before the coming light.'
He dipped the bread, then up and left,
the silver called his tune,
the shadows lengthened as he crept
beneath that weeping moon.

And soon, but in a garden now,
he led the enemy,
and with embracing arms he sealed
his final destiny.
When God had let go all but love
and come in human frame,
the incarnation spoke of grace
and now God gave the same.

Christ never lost control, but walked
into their arms, betrayed.
Yes, self-betrayal, gave himself,
as colleagues stood dismayed.
For now a life was offered up
with no dissenting voice.
Oh Judas kissed him, right enough,
but God had made the choice.

Metre: CMD

Suggested Tune: KINGSFOLD

Ignatian spirituality, in which we imagine ourselves as part of the Bible story and then reflect on what we feel and how we should respond, has become increasingly popular in recent years. This has opened the Bible in a fresh way for me. The drama that we enter becomes vivid, the characters real. And so we reflect on Judas and the illusion of power.

Between the clash of nations
compassion is denied,
and human love retarded
by strident human pride.
New crosses are erected,
new victims hang and die;
while Jesus looks in silence
and knows the reason why.

Unsettled by the hatred,
the heresy of fear,
God's children suffer daily,
through all they sense and hear.
Through each humiliation,
the ravages and pain,
God shares the world's derision,
is crucified again.

Within this present anguish,
as forces whirl and churn,
God give us hope to hold us
wherever life may turn.
Beyond the desecration,
when solitude is found,
may memories still bind us,
may each to each be bound.

Metre: 7.6.7.6.D.

Suggested Tunes: CRÜGER and PASSION CHORALE

The violence of the cross was religious and political in origin. The violence of the world is little different today. This hymn was written after hearing of a mother and children who were shot in a car in Israel. About the same time I had heard the author Jeanette Winterson talking about her life and writing.

Disturbed? Yes we have been disturbed.
Our faith in love is shaken.
As people twist the words we say
we feel we are forsaken.

Another felt the pain we feel,
for he was lost and friendless.
The ones he thought that he could trust
slept on while night seemed endless.

And in a courtyard, while the priests
were testing his intention,
a closer friend denied his love,
made clear his own dissension.

Beyond denial stood the cross;
crowds waited, heard him sighing:
'Forgive, they know not what they do'
– love's words, as love hung dying.

It seemed that God had left the stage,
the world had claimed its victim,
but love would live another day
and this is Jesus' maxim:

When people twist the words we say,
we feel we are forsaken,
but love will live another day,
and never will be shaken.

Metre: 8.7.8.7.

Suggested Tunes: CURBAR EDGE and ST COLUMBA (Anonymous Irish)

Identifying with Bible characters can help us to cope with our own experiences. I am personally aware of the pain that I feel when I say one thing and others twist or embellish what I have said until the meaning, and intention, are totally distorted. You begin to wonder just who you can trust. The story is not new …

Rising gloom surrounds the story,
Jesus moves towards the cross,
here Jerusalem is waiting,
favour swings from gain to loss.

Crowds had swarmed in adulation,
many came infused with hope.
Every person sought an outcome,
nothing seemed beyond his scope.

Zealots called for liberation,
sinners waited on his word,
children ran with palms to meet him,
felt affirmed by what they heard.

Other people simply bustled,
thought their lives beyond reproach,
when the Lord came riding humbly,
hardly noticed his approach.

In the temple, tables turning,
those in power were disabused
as he showed the way to worship
for the poor, despised, abused.

Choices faced him in the garden,
prayer was dry, betrayal lurked;
while his closest friends were sleeping,
human evil waited, worked.

What is left? Some trumped-up charges?
Self-conceit? Religious hate?
Here the Christ still stands before us –
time for judgement ... crosses wait.

Metre: 8.7.8.7.

Suggested Tunes: ADORATION (Hunt) and GALILEE (Jude)

This reflection on the Easter story, moving from Palm Sunday to Good Friday, was written at a workshop on hymns, held in April 2004 at Holland House, Cropthorne, near Pershore, and run by Mike and Carolyn Sanderson.

Bleakly broken, face of sorrow,
lowliness worn like a gown.
Borne with dignity, your anguished,
thorn encrusted, tarnished crown.

Lamb they call you, lunging blindly
after thoughts that strew your way,
never really understanding
all the things you do or say.

Now you hang while they despise you,
breaking what they cannot hold,
'God forgive', how you surprised them:
'God forgive', such love untold.

Metre: 8.7.8.7.

Suggested Tune: ST ANDREW

There is still a point in describing crucifixion. However, this is no longer a 'wondrous cross' in which we glory, but a real execution. These words echo something of Isaiah 53.

Stark outline of three crosses on a hill,
a silhouette, a shadow, stark and still;
a crass, barbaric, savage way to kill.

Sharp agony, the bodies writhe until,
in twisting, turning, they have had their fill.
Unnumbered hours measure out this ill.

Such love; the words are masochistic, shrill.
Such irony to script, declare, distil
what happened on that day. Was this God's will?

We watch life ebb, Christ takes the bitterest pill,
as blood runs cold, while senses numb and chill.
The sign of love, God's greatest gift and skill.

Metre: 10 10 10

Suggested Tune: LÖWENSTERN

Ever since the death of my son, I have found Good Friday immensely hard to bear. I used to think that those who avoided Good Friday worship were avoiding the pain, only wanting the pleasure and celebration of Easter Sunday. Now I have greater sympathy with those who would avoid it. For some the images are just too real, too fresh. I do not believe that the way to address this is by sanitising the reality. The sentimentality of another age is of little help. Neither for me is the theologising which tries to make sense of a simple, sordid, politically motivated death. Rather, I would want to draw parallels with the world in which we live, to understand that we are still politically motivated, still flawed human beings living in a real world. In that context I want to make sense of the cross.

M. von Löwenstern (1594–1648)

Stark____ out – line of three cross – es on a hill,

a sil – hou – ette, a sha – dow, stark and still;

a crass, bar – ba – ric, sa – vage way___ to kill.

62 He owned little, sought for nothing

He owned little, sought for nothing,
drained of all his power.
Sadly hanging, crossed, forgotten,
love was going sour.

Christ was spurned, his friends had scattered,
leaving him to die.
Desolation now his consort,
shadows cloud the sky.

Did this drama change creation?
What of those who saw?
Here a soldier found a saviour.
Mary's grief was raw.

Later people spoke of beauty:
strange theology.
Elegance was torn, distorted:
love nailed to a tree.

Death changed nothing. But the dawning
of a glorious hope
blazed through those who saw in Jesus
love of boundless scope.

Metre: 8.5.8.5.

Suggested Tune: GOD, YOU HOLD ME (see page 25)

The more I reflect on the cross of Jesus, the more I see hope in the way he faced it. Aside from any divine attribution here is a man who is worth emulating, whose example is worth following.

We watch him die

See! Torn, tormented, images
that scream as flesh is torn to death,
the clouds of gas, the sighs of life,
where God loves nonetheless.

I cry to see humanity
born on this stage of tears and grief,
where life is cheap and sliced by shards,
and love finds no relief.

Is there no resurrection end,
no way beyond this hurt and pain,
no way for grace to offer love,
no way to joy again?

The hands that once were pierced by nails,
still calloused, scarred by splintered wood,
reach into fire, and hold in hell,
are faithful, strong and good.

Metre: 8.8.8.6.

Suggested Tune: MISERICORDIA (Smart)

The human example of Jesus begins to make sense in the midst of the horror of war and our continued inhumanity. Any sense of incarnation adds to that, but Jesus's humanity is of value in itself.

I wrote this text at an exhibition of Methodist Modern Art at Hope in Everton (Liverpool Hope University) in September 2002, after hearing a talk by Peter Forsaith, the curator of the collection.

The hands of God held fast to love
when slammed against a cross of wood.
God's love would never dissipate,
nor ever loose the grasp of good.

The longing, loving eyes of Christ
looked as he hung and suffered there;
and all the suffering of the world
distilled to passion in that care.

The poor who looked with longing eyes,
who met their saviour's steady gaze,
knew in that moment all the love
that touched their pain through tear-filled haze.

And still we look and hang upon
a saviour's dying care and grace;
and still we see the love of God
effulgent in a human face.

Metre: LM

Suggested Tunes: NÜRNBERG and WAREHAM

Hands have a particular significance for me. As an artist, my son worked with his hands. After his death in a road accident it was only his hands that we could hold. So Jesus's hands have become a focus for my meditation in a way that is completely authentic.

The heavy stone had rolled away
and through the morning light,
the women saw an empty tomb
and, terrified, took flight.

What happened in those latter days
to loosen fear–tied tongues?
We only know grief turned to joy
and singing filled their lungs.

Their utter grief was real enough,
the record rings as true,
and only time will tell if grief
can change for me and you.

That is our hope, but faith is hard
to grasp, or reconcile
with all that life has brought our way,
and joy is not our style.

Come to the centre of our pain
and sow the seeds of praise,
that, not denying anything,
your love might calm our days.

Metre: CM

Suggested Tune: GRÄFENBERG (NUN DANKET ALL)

The immediate response to the empty tomb is not one of celebration of resurrection but rather one of horror and fear. Mark's Gospel tells of women running from the tomb, terrified. That is real enough. When I have been in the depths of grief I have not wanted, or been able, to cry 'Alleluia!'. Neither have I been able to consider the possibility of resurrection. That could only come much later. An earlier version of this text, with the first line 'The sharpened chill, the flower-strewn tomb', was published in 'Let Justice Roll Down', an anthology of texts for Lent, Holy Week and Easter compiled by Geoffrey Duncan (Canterbury Press, 2003).

66 When neighbours turn and look away

When neighbours turn and look away,
when friends deride and words are curt,
God meets us, crosses to our side,
anoints our wounds and heals our hurt.

And can the hands that formed the earth
reach out to comfort humankind?
The strong, creative love of God,
compassion's source, will soothe and bind.

God would not turn or look away
from those who sigh, from those who bleed;
God comes and reaches those who cry,
forsaken in their hour of need.

That cross, a sign of cruelty,
raised up to signal all the earth,
as God was hanging crucified
Christ's love affirmed our human worth.

No circumstance destroys God's love.
God feels the silent words we pray.
God suffers still, and shares our pain.
This parent will not turn away.

Metre: LM

Suggested Tunes: MELCOMBE and DUNEDIN

A modern hymn speaks of God looking away at the time of his son's crucifixion. That doesn't feel theologically or scripturally right to me. There is a conundrum at the centre of Christian credal theology. To begin with it is God who died on the cross. But to make sense of the incarnation we name Jesus as God's son. This is nothing new. We read it in scripture.

    Then, when Jesus cries, 'My God, my God, why have you forsaken me?' that cry of dereliction is to a God in whom Jesus believes most profoundly, and whom scripture elsewhere would affirm would never actually turn away, though that may be his and our perception.

We watch him die

Our words have built such calvaries
while Christ befriends the very ones
that we would judge and cast away.
He makes them neighbours. Love will stay.

We wander after our desires
and build our empires out of greed,
while with the lost and destitute
Christ makes a pact. He's resolute.

We change with every charm and chance
that seem to offer proud rewards,
while he is constant, offering care
that will not fail. You see his stare?

That is the judgement, not belief
in minute details, magic acts;
but how we live and love with those
outside the walls. The ones he chose.

Metre: LM

Suggested Tunes: ELIM (HESPERUS) AND WOODWORTH

Coming from the point at which metaphysical ideas meant nothing at all to me, although the person of Jesus was still supremely significant, I needed either to make sense of Christianity or to set it aside. Either Jesus was still important or not. If not, then there was nothing left for me in this faith which I had proclaimed for many years, and no point in staying with the church that had given me solace and my living. So I began to seek more deeply and to question more insistently. And when I had sufficient courage, I shared in hymns and in sermons what I was discovering. This hymn comes from that process, and it was written after reading a chapter of 'Doubt and Loves' by Richard Holloway (Canongate Books, 2001).

Raw rage, the counterblast to love,
that tore the mind, that ravaged flesh,
remains to crucify again –
is still as blind, is just as fresh.

Repairing life, asserting love,
forgiveness hung and life was drained,
but through the mist undying grace
survived, though human hell remained.

The focus of those clouded eyes
retains the power to claim our gaze,
and still undying love sustains
God's people in this hate-filled maze.

Metre: LM

Suggested Tunes: MAINZER and OLIVE'S BROW

Hatred has not been banished from the world in some magical way because of the crucifixion or resurrection, but perhaps what happened two thousand years ago can show us something of the love in which we're held.

Reflect on all it means

How can we stand, ignoring each injustice?
How can we watch in silence, never learn
that making peace will bring the need to suffer,
absorbing hatred on the cross of love?

Here is the challenge facing every Christian:
to raise again the cross on which Christ died;
no metaphor, no easy resurrection,
our cup, like his, is not an easy draught.

So can we die, yes, offer no resistance,
save that of love, our lives poured out as grace;
to freely proffer hope where life is desperate,
to raise the dying, comfort those who hate?

Metre: 11.10.11.10.

Suggested Tune: INTERCESSOR

Faith becomes very practical when you look at the human Jesus. If you have any belief in what he did, then you are forced to act, to speak and to write, and to accept the consequences. One example of this was the case of the peace activist Norman Kember, who was taken hostage in Iraq in 2005, while trying to live by his Christian pacifist principles in that troubled country. These words were written as President George W. Bush supported a new scheme put forward by Israeli Prime Minister Ariel Sharon to resettle Palestinians and maintain Israeli settlements.

To move beyond this certainty
where all is safe, each way is known;
to enter into mystery
takes all the faith that we can own.

To cast off from security
beyond the shore, to reach the race,
where life can strain integrity,
will challenge hope, require God's grace.

But in the midst of tidal change,
the shift and drift, this swirling strife,
we'll never reach beyond love's range,
God shares each pitch and toss of life.

Metre: LM

Suggested Tunes: FESTUS (Freylinghausen) and CORNISH

Faith is needed if we are to be as Jesus in the world in which we live. Here, nothing is certain or secure.

Lives are the currency spent in war's carnage,
self-interest blinding the people in power.
Reckless decisions are made without wisdom;
God, through your love, hold us back from this hour.

Nation meets nation but language is twisted,
lies clothed as truth, while ill poses as good;
all that now matters, it seems, is the 'victory',
bought through the spilling of innocent blood.

God of the innocent, dying unheeded,
God of Gethsemane, Christ of the cross,
hear the world's pleading, then offer your loving,
hands scarred with nails reach to share in our loss.

Then in our dying, God, bring resurrection,
lift us and save us, renew and forgive;
through devastation where meaning lies broken,
bring us new love and a reason to live.

Metre: 11.10.11.10.

Suggested Tunes: STEWARDSHIP and WAS LEBET

In the world it is so easy to be carried along by political rhetoric, and yet it is here the greatest sin is committed – against the Holy Spirit – where our values become so distorted that we see good as evil and evil as good. This hymn was written during the preparations for war against Iraq, when Tony Blair, the Prime Minister, was accused by a member of the Cabinet, Clare Short, of being reckless. The text received an 'Honorable Mention' from the Hymn Society in the United States and Canada.

So bleak with possibility,
bare branches reach for hope,
a promise in this barren time
of love of boundless scope.

We look beyond this season's end,
through winter's lengthened night,
to longer days, and new-found growth,
the cross no more a blight.

Each healing hand, each watchful eye,
each grief or joy we share,
lives out that resurrection love,
our calling and our care.

Metre: CM

Suggested Tune: WESTMINSTER

As we move in terms of our faith from Good Friday to Easter Sunday we mirror the Easter story. Celebration is not always immediate; and, humanly, resurrection is often mediated by ordinary people who see our pain or reach out a hand to help.

In the garden, walking, weeping,
Mary came at break of dawn.
All the sorrow, all the anguish
made her figure lost, forlorn.

All the fragrance of that garden
couldn't take away her fear;
coming through the dancing shadows,
sunshine could not calm or cheer.

In the corner of the garden
was the tomb where he'd been laid.
Her intention was to hold him,
feel again the love he gave.

Now she saw the tomb was empty,
heard a gardener call her name,
turning round she saw him, Jesus,
one who'd reached her through her shame.

Sunshine cut through clouds of mourning,
for his death had come and gone,
silencing the dirge of sorrow,
now she'd sing a sweeter song.

Metre: 8.7.8.7.

Suggested Tune: OMNI DIE

My quest for a human Jesus has led me to look at biblical passages, particularly those of the gospels, as narratives about real people in real situations. I suppose this began for me in the contributions I and many other writers made to 'Story Song' (Stainer & Bell and The Methodist Church Division of Education and Youth, 1993). The process has become more urgent and necessary. This hymn was written for Carson Cooman's tune TUCKERNUCK. It was published in the 'Methodist Recorder' in March 2002 and first sung at Bispham, Clowes and Orrell Methodist Churches in the Orrell and Lamberhead Green Circuit on Easter Sunday, 31 March 2002.

What is it charms our minds
and makes us see his face,
as breaking bread he shares a meal
with us within this place?

We'd walked along the way
and talked of what had passed.
Our eyes were blind to who he was,
how could we break this fast?

Emmaus comes in sight,
we walk within its walls,
then coming to our place of rest
we pause as darkness falls.

Then suddenly it's light,
the scales fall from our eyes;
this bright, divine epiphany
not one of us denies.

We see him face to face,
we recognise the Lord,
our harmony has been restored,
his note completes the chord.

Metre: SM

Suggested Tunes: GARELOCHSIDE and ST MICHAEL (Crotch)

Having begun to explore the first Easter Sunday morning, I have in this hymn written imaginatively about the walk to Emmaus.

75   Playful God, you laugh and dance

JOYFUL GOD   *Marlene Phillips (1933–)*

Playful God, you laugh and dance _____ at e - very in - di - ca - tion that
we have caught a glimpse, a _____ glance of ma - gic in cre - a - tion.

Playful God, you laugh and dance
at every indication
that we have caught a glimpse, a glance
of magic in creation.

Tearful God, you weep and mourn,
you share our desolation;
in every doubt, in pain and grief,
we need your consolation.

Joyful God, we praise your name
in every situation.
Your love will even live through death,
you promise resurrection.

Mighty God, creative heart
and source of our elation,
accept our praise, our lives, our all,
our ceaseless adoration.

Words and Music © Copyright 2006 Stainer & Bell Ltd

Metre: 7.7.8.7.

Suggested Tune: JOYFUL GOD

The exploration of the essence of the gospel need not be all heavy going. Images which picture God in a variety of human guises can help. A belief in incarnation makes such images legitimate. This hymn was one of two joyful resurrection texts written within three days of each other at the beginning of December 2004!

76   When being is threatened and life is abused

When being is threatened and life is abused,
when lives are devalued and names are confused;
then here in the terror, the triumph of pain,
you come to renew, to rebuild us again.

Before we had started you held us in grace,
but life has denied us both status and place;
society names us, determines our role,
affirms or derides us, belittles, makes whole.

But love is not neutral, with justice it's dressed.
You hold and enfold us, still treasured and blessed.
You judge the oppressor, you lift up the poor,
your bias is certain, your judgement is sure.

And so in that knowledge we work for release.
We challenge oppression, incarnate God's peace.
Through us, through our practice, God works in this age,
establishing justice across the world's stage.

Metre: 11 11.11 11.

Suggested Tunes: DATCHET and ST DENIO

Anthony Reddie, a research fellow at the Queen's Foundation for Ecumenical Theological Education in Birmingham, and a consultant in black theological studies for the British Methodist Church, spoke about black theology at my place of work, The Partnership for Theological Education, in Manchester. I was moved by the pictures he painted and the images he addressed, and again I tried to make sense of what I was hearing by writing it out in verse.

Meet the risen Jesus

On Friday, when the sky was dark,
disciples fled in fright
and dazed, through Saturday, they wait
the dawn of Sunday's light.

From dull despair to blazing light,
from agony and death,
God's people sought for grace and hope,
and for the Spirit's breath.

The silent waking of the Christ
brought all the world to praise,
as death was done and life reborn
with hope for all our days.

That hope returns with each new year,
the prompt for faith's rebirth
and brighter than a thousand suns
God's glory flames on earth!

As new life forces through the earth,
the world is sprung with green,
and all creation rings again
as joy is sung and seen.

Metre: CM

Suggested Tunes: ST BOTOLPH (Slater) and FORGIVE OUR SINS (DETROIT)

In spite of my searching and questioning I still find something compelling in the traditional images of Easter, and I return to them.

Hear how our praises rang!
Our songs of hope ran high,
but that was in another time,
now darkness clouds the sky.

The tears that we will cry,
the shroud of grief we wear,
are evidence of sundered love,
of all we have to bear.

As Mary wept for Christ,
while grief was sharp and raw,
so now we feel akin with her
through all we felt, and saw.

God sow a seed of hope,
and give us, through your grace,
the merest essence of your love
to resurrect our faith.

Metre: SM

Suggested Tunes: GARELOCHSIDE and FESTAL SONG

If the story of the resurrection is a myth, in the right sense of that word, then its application and relevance are timeless. If it is just a matter of history or arcane theology, then it relates little to our common, everyday experience. An earlier version of this text, with the first line 'Alleluias echoed', was published in 'Let Justice Roll Down', an anthology of texts for Lent, Holy Week and Easter compiled by Geoffrey Duncan (Canterbury Press, 2003).

Holy wonder, grace unbounded,
joy of heaven, born to die;
you have treasured love, confounded
human hatred, arcane lie.

You have crossed each vain assertion
made by those constrained by pride;
flooring those whose failed exertion
sought to banish or deride.

Now we wake and, healed of shyness,
hail the dawn with newborn hope;
nurturing the loving kindness
that will give our souls new scope.

Metre: 8.7.8.7.

Suggested Tunes: WRAYSBURY and RATHBUN

For resurrection to be real today it has to be lived today. We need to live as though it is possible to begin again and again, even after death.

Here in the feast and the folly, our future,
founded in love, will continue to grow;
here, where we learn both to comfort and nurture,
God is the centre of all we can know.

Then we would hear the divine invitation,
'Leave all behind you and follow my way;
I will walk with you through love's re-creation.'
Christ our companion through every new day.

Now we would follow without hesitation,
joy of our lives, both the path and the goal.
Spirit of grace and the hope of each person,
meeting our brokenness, making us whole.

Metre: 11.10.11.10.

Suggested Tunes: EPIPHANY HYMN and WAS LEBET

I have had a recurring sense of call throughout my life, ever since I first felt a need to find out about God. The call has not always been in the same direction. Sometimes it has been worked out intellectually. On occasion it has come through another person's suggestion, and there have been moments when it was a matter of feeling or compulsion. This sense of vocation has sometimes held behind it a selfish motivation. Always, when it has been real, it has brought healing or encouragement, energy or renewal. There have been times when 'to follow' has seemed like folly, and others have warned me off what I was going to do or say, afraid of what the consequences might be. It was, perhaps, not much different for the first disciples.

We would be an Easter people
living resurrection now,
making all those years of promise
real, as Jesus shows us how.

Meeting Mary, Jesus loved her,
calling to her by her name.
Those who need the love of Jesus
we will welcome just the same.

'Peace be with you' was Christ's greeting
to the ones who'd let him die.
May our greeting be as gracious
to the ones who'd spurn our cry.

Doubting Thomas was confounded;
Jesus loved him in his doubt.
Help us welcome saint and sceptic
as we work your purpose out.

Let us live the resurrection
in each time, in every place.
Let us live as Easter people,
true to Jesus' boundless grace.

Metre: 8.7.8.7.

Suggested Tunes: SHARON (HALTON HOLGATE) and CHARLESTOWN

Easter People is the title of an annual, seasonal evangelical gathering begun in the UK by the Rev. Dr Rob Frost. It is also the name used by St Augustine for those who followed Jesus. When we respond to the call of God we become like Jesus; arguably we become Easter people. That may not always be as easy or as comfortable as it sounds. This hymn was first published in 'Let Justice Roll Down', an anthology of texts for Lent, Holy Week and Easter compiled by Geoffrey Duncan (Canterbury Press, 2003) and has since been used for a communion service at Easter People.

Jesus left them. God empowered them.
Spirit flamed from age to age.
And that spirit can't be silenced;
now's our time to take the stage.

Every nation that had gathered
was invited on that day;
and the spirit still unites us:
Pentecost has come to stay.

As disciples came together
they would hold a common purse,
share their meals, their wealth and praises,
to the world they seemed perverse.

Still, today, we'll trace that pattern,
working for the good of all,
in our politics and preaching,
faithful to the gospel's call.

Metre: 8.7.8.7.

Suggested Tunes: STAPLEGROVE and BENG-LI

The resurrection of Jesus without the ascension would present a problem. What happens to Jesus next? Does he die again? What initiates the church if Jesus is still there? Whether or not we take the story literally, Jesus has to be removed from the scene before the church can be born.

Great prophet of pity, subversive in love,
unsettle our comfort, divert and reprove;
that, moved from self-interest, and shielded from pride,
we might yet embody the gifts of your bride.

Oh raise up your people and fit them to care,
for all who are lonely or lost in despair.
The reed that is bending, the wick that burns low,
through grace and persistence, God, help them to grow.

From each generation, race, colour or creed,
Christ, gather together, united by need,
the ones that you value, and God, may we find,
in spite of ourselves that your welcome is kind.

Metre: 11 11.11 11.

Suggested Tune: ST DENIO

Muslims think of Jesus as a prophet. Much of what he said and did was prophetic in the theological sense. Jesus points to the way we should be in the presence of God, and singles out those who, though they think themselves holy and righteous, are hypocrites. Jesus undermines our false values and challenges every aspect of our lives. The more I learn about Jesus the more I want to know, and the further I know myself to be from the ideal he presents. Yet I cling to some words of Frederick Faber, the nineteenth-century clergyman and hymn writer, which he addressed to an order of religious brothers, the Wilfridians, that he'd established: 'Do not fear the judgement, you will find it very gentle, very kindly, very safe.' I pray that it is so. The phrase 'great prophet of pity' is found on page 198 of 'Doubts and Loves' by Richard Holloway (Canongate Books, 2001).

Here we meet to seek God's purpose,
catch a glimpse of given grace,
find a way to mirror goodness
in this present time and place;

walk with love, the future beckons,
now we need to deepen trust,
recognise a common purpose,
mutual care, less cut and thrust.

Best of all, our God is with us
as we frame each concrete scheme,
as we answer human questions,
as we try to live a dream.

© Copyright 2006 Stainer & Bell Ltd

Metre: 8.7.8.7.

Suggested Tunes: ST CATHERINE (Jones) and GALILEE (Jude)

Christians, from the day of Pentecost onwards, have met together. When they have met they have not always agreed. Life isn't very different now in my experience. We still argue and debate, still have mixed motives and hidden agendas. This hymn was written for a meeting of Christians. The first line of the last stanza was originally 'Best of all is God is with us', words attributed to John Wesley on his deathbed. Methodists might like to use that variation to the text.

We cannot privatise God's grace
and in our hearts we know it.
The love of God is ours, it's free,
we know that we must show it.

The neighbour that becomes a friend
becomes a gift God's given,
the barrier that's broken down,
a clearer path to heaven.

So, take my hand and let us dance
the freedom steps from prison,
a choreography of love
where joy is no illusion.

Metre: 8.7.8.7.

Suggested Tunes: DOMINUS REGIT ME and ST COLUMBA (Anonymous Irish)

I remember an evangelical chorus, 'It only takes a spark to get a fire going', which had the line 'you want to pass it on' – God's love, that is. Keeping God's love to ourselves never made sense and it still doesn't, but passing it on sometimes means allying ourselves with people with whom we'd rather not associate.

Seek to follow in his steps   95

PILGRIM TUNE

Alan Prosser (1948–)

Jauntily

Where are you go - ing? God on - ly knows. Walk on pil - grim, pil - grim sing. It's

not where you're go - ing. It's how you are chang - ing. Come on pil - grim! Pil - grim sing!

Where are you going? God only knows.
Walk on pilgrim, pilgrim sing.
It's not where you're going.
It's how you are changing.
Come on pilgrim! Pilgrim sing!

Walk with another, walk on as one.
Come on pilgrim, pilgrim sing.
Your friends will walk with you,
and others will join you.
Walk on pilgrims! Pilgrims sing!

Walk midst the water, walk through the fire.
Walk on pilgrims, pilgrims sing.
Your God will walk with you,
your God will protect you.
Come on pilgrims! Pilgrims sing!

Seek to follow in his steps

Climb up the mountain, follow the sun.
Come on pilgrims, pilgrims sing.
The leaves turn to auburn
to welcome the autumn.
Walk on pilgrims! Pilgrims sing!

God is behind you, God is ahead.
Walk on pilgrims, pilgrims sing.
The winter may chill you,
the spring will enchant you.
Come on pilgrims! Pilgrims sing!

Summer is coming, spirit of joy.
Come on pilgrims, pilgrims sing.
Then dance as you travel,
sing 'hail resurrection'.
Walk on pilgrims! Pilgrims sing!

Metre: 9.7.6.6.7.

Suggested Tune: PILGRIM TUNE

We respond to God's call without knowing where it will lead. These words were written for a Bispham Methodist Church weekend at Low Bank Ground, Coniston, on the theme of pilgrimage. The tune 'with a medieval lilt' was written by Alan Prosser.

We live with constant changes
within God's love and grace,
where challenge would direct us,
or just within this place.

We follow dancing footsteps,
and in them find our own,
or, moulded by a potter,
our clay is shaped and thrown.

We find the way before us,
the way we ought to be;
begun, continued, ended,
within love's ecstasy.

Metre: 7.6.7.6.

Suggested Tune: CHRISTUS DER IST MEIN LEBEN

Sometimes in my Christian pilgrimage I've moved literally from one place to another. At others I've changed or grown spiritually but stayed physically in the same place. The important thing for all of us, I believe, is to find where we ought to be, the place where we can best use the gifts that God has given us. These words were written after hearing Fr Paul Daly speaking on Roman Catholic ministerial formation at a conference on Methodist ministerial formation held in 2004 at Manchester's Hartley Victoria College, England.

Spirited dancer, a pantomime figure,
comic, distorted, misused and abused;
never expedient, yet working with rigour,
seemingly foolish yet never confused.

Crying the wilderness down on your shoulders,
offering pedants the cool time of day;
I would dance with you, by paths or rough boulders,
willing to enter the fun or the fray.

Now in my cowardice, fear, apprehension,
sharing the life that you've given to me;
help me to put away pride and pretension,
learn in your footsteps the way to be free.

Metre: 11.10.11.10.

Suggested Tunes: QUEDLINBURG and WAS LEBET

Jesus is not easy to follow. St Paul talks of us being 'fools for Christ'. I imagine Jesus as, metaphorically, a dancer or a pantomime figure, comic, the butt of derision. This text was first published in 'Let Justice Roll Down', an anthology of texts for Lent, Holy Week and Easter compiled by Geoffrey Duncan (Canterbury Press, 2003).

Seek to follow in his steps

Now, at a point in time,
we gather in this place
to offer all we have and are,
responding to God's grace.

One body called by God,
with many gifts and skills,
affirming those with whom we serve,
discerning what God wills.

The laying on of hands
accompanied by prayer
we use to point out those we sense
are drawn, by God, to care.

And others still are called
to break the bread, to share,
to help us join a gracious meal
and find God's presence there.

We celebrate God's call,
anticipate the feast,
where all God's people rise affirmed,
the greatest and the least.

Metre: SM

Suggested Tune: SHERE

For me worship began in the open air with real images of beauty all around me. Nature is a sacrament for me, in the sense that it mediates God's grace, puts me in touch with God. But I serve within a Christian denomination that understands how God can be met when we share bread and wine in a service of communion. I have also found God here. This hymn was written in 2004 at a conference on Methodist ministerial formation held at Hartley Victoria College.

Sing alleluia! Celebrate
the gifts that God has given:
the charismatic marks of love
anticipating heaven.

Sing alleluia! Celebrate
the skills that have been taught,
the dormant craft that God awakes,
the faith that has been sought.

Sing alleluia! Celebrate,
cooperate with grace,
as gathered here we offer God
ourselves within this place.

Sing alleluia! Celebrate
with those that we ordain
to work with us, to do God's will
through joy, or yet in pain.

Sing alleluia! Celebrate,
go in the spirit's power,
and as one body live God's love
in this and every hour.

Metre: CM

Suggested Tunes: UNIVERSITY and MCKEE

Churches in their different ways mark people off and give them roles. So, one person is ordained a bishop, while another is given the job of organising a flower rota.

Amazing creativity:
a wizardry with words,
a potter working at a wheel,
a 'twitcher' watching birds.
A soaring operatic song,
a gift with what is said,
the choreography of life,
a gardener in her shed.

A plotter of the stars by night,
a dance to swing or sway,
conception of computer games,
the scripting of a play.
A story or a parable,
a captivating tale,
the craft and skill an engineer
might use with road or rail.

The painter or the sculptor's craft
in representing form,
the plumber, or the scientist
predicting quake or storm.
Each gift and talent that we see,
each spirit-driven skill,
provides a chance for partnership
with God's creative will.

Metre: CMD

Suggested Tune: KINGSFOLD

I have grown to believe that part of what we should be doing is working with creation, working with God. And there are so many ways in which this can happen. I was asked by Brenda Bibby, then Senior Steward at Bispham Methodist Church in Billinge, Wigan, to write a hymn or song about gifts and talents. I reflected on J. K. Rowling's prodigious output of Harry Potter novels and this text was the outcome. In the United Kingdom a 'twitcher' is a birdwatcher.

In every life there's need for space,
a room to echo, full of love,
not close confined or limited
by earth beneath or sky above.

This space within or round ourselves
where God is found, where quietness dwells,
is where our source of peace resides,
from here all sense of comfort wells.

We feel around, within this place,
security, we ease our pace,
and while we pause to be renewed
we know God's love, God's healing grace.

Metre: LM

Suggested Tune: O WALY WALY

Having found my first place of worship to be under open skies, I have also found places of solitude and fellowship in many other situations. In 2003, in Christ's and Notre Dame Chapel, Liverpool Hope University College, while waiting for my PhD viva, I wrote these words.

93   Keep on bothering God!

Keep on bothering God!
God has not gone away.
Of course you may not hear that voice,
or what it has to say.

Keep on bothering God!
Your wayward prayers can sing
a loud lament, a cry for hope,
the needs that you must bring.

Keep on bothering God!
Persist, for God will hear,
and hearing listen to your cry
and wipe away your fear.

Keep on bothering God!
And listen for that call,
however long you have to wait,
respond and give your all.

Keep on bothering God!
Each bring your bothering praise,
a praise that never will be stopped
through all your living days.

© Copyright 2006 Stainer & Bell Ltd

Metre: SM

Suggested Tune: BOTHERING GOD

Prayer, talking with God however informally, is often our first point of real contact with the divine. Sometimes this conversation can be a shout of anguish, swearing, as we shout 'O God!' when something goes badly wrong. It may not sound like prayer, it may not be meant as prayer, but it is certainly meant! Jesus spoke of the need to be persistent in prayer. Jenny Canham, a member of the Hymn Society of Great Britain and Ireland, asked for a hymn with the opening line 'Keep bothering God'! In Australia, members of the clergy are known as 'God-botherers'.

BOTHERING GOD

June Baker (1936–)

Keep on both-er-ing God! God has not gone a-way. Of course you may not hear that voice, or what it has to say.

In lives of worship

The doors are closed, the music hushed
yet, as we bow in prayer,
the spirit moves beyond these walls
to those still left out there.

Across the street, around the world,
our neighbours cry again;
so easy for the likes of us
to just ignore their pain.

God give us courage in this life
to put aside our greed,
to mirror Jesus' deeds and words,
to share with those in need.

© Copyright 2006 Stainer & Bell Ltd

Metre: CM

Suggested Tunes: CAITHNESS and MARTYRDOM

When we worship I am always conscious of those who are not there. This has been particularly heightened for me when I have ministered to congregations in places where, for safety, doors are closed or even locked during services. And there is a metaphor in the 'locked door', for we close other doors to people by our words or our attitudes, excluding those who, perhaps, most need God's loving grace and acceptance. It is a good job that the 'delivery' of God's grace does not depend on the church!

What, in this world, is the point of our worship,
raising our hands and our voices in praise?
God in the centre, we serve in our neighbours,
these are the ones we should value and raise.

Words are ephemeral, empty and pointless,
praises are hollow, our faith just a mask,
up to the point that in kindness, with justice,
we can respond to our God-given task.

Ritual and rhythm, precision of practice,
all that we do in the worship of God,
this must be mirrored each day in our living,
walking in paths that the powerless have trod.

Metre: 11.10.11.10.

Suggested Tune: IN THE BEGINNING GOD PLAYED WITH THE PLANETS (see page 3)

Many 'modern' choruses speak of lifting Jesus up. Aside from the question of whether that is even a theological possibility, when I hear these words I am reminded of the words in 1 John 4:20: '... those who do not love a brother or sister whom they have seen, cannot love God whom they have not seen' (NRSV). Rabbi Lionel Blue once observed that if worship doesn't make us better people, more kind to each other, there's not a lot of point to it. For me worship must always reach beyond the church into the world outside.

Moved by music, offer praise,
hear the loud, triumphant chord,
soft cadenza, rising swell,
harmony in one accord.

Celebrate the builder's skill,
voicing pipes that others play.
Let our chorus soar beyond
earthbound tunes in heaven's way.

Pull the stops out, feel the sound:
flute and diapason pour
music that will charm our hearts,
raise our hopes, engender awe.

When the last resounding chord
echoes till the air is still,
may the memory of this day
energise both heart and will.

May the music that we live,
notes set on the staff of life,
speak of harmony and love,
ending discord, fear and strife.

Metre: 7.7.7.7.

Suggested Tunes: EMMA and SONG 13 (CANTERBURY)

As our worship has a purpose and intention beyond the walls of the church, then even the dedication of a church organ ought to point us to a world beyond.

Soft wounds of brush on canvas,
the scraping of a knife,
the match and mix of colour,
will give a picture life;

and God carved in millennia,
through geologic time,
the pattern and the picture,
divinity's design.

With hesitance we follow,
we mimic in our ways
the sculptor of creation
and, through this, offer praise.

Metre: 7.6.7.6.

Suggested Tune: CHERRY TREE CAROL

Human beings are immensely creative but that creativity is a sharing in God's creativity. It seems to me that this has two consequences for Christians. It should be a guard against arrogance and it should also make us careful about what we seek to create. Our creativity should always have a loving purpose. An earlier version of this text was published in 'A Place for Us', an anthology of texts compiled by Geoffrey Duncan (Granary Press, 2004).

Timbers torn, while tiles lie broken,
see foundations swept away;
bricks dislodged, while stones are shattered,
human lives in disarray;
chaos rules, while God seems absent,
love lies bleeding on the ground;
dust is caught in shafts of sunlight,
crying is the only sound.

Here amid this devastation
we can build and live again;
here within our human anguish,
God is sharing in our pain.
Where our graceless intervention
brings destruction, death and war,
we will work to ease the torment
rather than redress the score.

Here where children have no future,
here where adults grasp for food,
we will share the gospel's goodness,
straighten lives that have been skewed.
We will work beside our neighbours,
offer love we could not own,
raising shelters for the homeless,
building houses, stone by stone.

Metre: 8.7.8.7.D.

Suggested Tune: ABBOT'S LEIGH

As my Christian understanding has developed and I have explored what this has meant, I have found myself more and more involved with issues of justice. These have ranged from AIDS/HIV to my involvement with the Methodist Peace Fellowship. My writing has given expression to my thoughts and has, hopefully, enabled people to gain different perspectives through poetry and hymns. As I have written about grief and tragedy, I have had to address the questions they raise and our response to them. On reflection this is all part of a continuing personal process of trying to understand God better, something that I have always pursued in verse. This text reflects on our need to respond as Christians to natural devastation.

God's peace is not beyond our grasp,
but there in every glance
that looks into a stranger's face
and takes a Christ-like chance.

God's peace is fashioned by the will,
the choice to love or hate;
that choice is ours, to reconcile,
to damage or create.

The freedom that we exercise,
decisions that we make,
are our responsibility,
define the path we take.

So everything is down to us
throughout this teeming earth;
to take again the path to war,
or bring God's rule to birth;

To follow in the steps of Christ,
to trust that through God's grace,
the peace we cannot comprehend
can grow within this place.

Metre: CM

Suggested Tune: MARTYRDOM

The living out of our faith has many practical consequences which sometimes challenge us to prove by our witness that the world is wrong. Peace is possible, but it is also costly.

Evil has no axis
outside the human mind,
immune to pain and suffering,
that's heartless, sick or blind.

Those we seek to label
are human, just like us.
We show our inhumanity
when language is unjust.

Christ is in our neighbour,
but hatred screens our sight,
distorting whom we ought to see;
compassion's put to flight.

God, sow seeds of conscience,
then nurture what's been sown
within the soil of our remorse,
till love is fully grown.

Metre: SM

Suggested Tune: SUTTON COMMON

George W. Bush, in his 2002 presidential State of the Union address, used the phrase 'axis of evil' when speaking of North Korea, Iran and Iraq. They were perceived by him to be potential terrorist threats following the destruction of the World Trade Center on 11 September 2001. It is natural for me to respond to such statements, to counter them. In the event, no weapons of mass destruction were found in Iraq, and the war there has been widely regarded as illegal.

Help us tread the paths of justice,
help us walk the ways of grace,
where your love and judgement mingle
in each paradox we face.

Show us ways of right discernment,
give us clarity of thought,
offer purity of vision,
let your righteousness be sought.

Here in this day's generation
fear and prejudice must melt;
strong in justice and compassion,
may the love of Christ be felt.

Metre: 8.7.8.7.

Suggested Tunes: LAUS DEO (Redhead) and EMMAUS (Sedio)

The moment we speak of mercy and love it is easy to be challenged to take notice of justice. Justice and mercy are not irreconcilable opposites, but it is easy to be swayed in one way or another, and as Christians we must continually live within this tension.

Today every person must face the decision
to welcome another with dancing and joy,
or offer the judgement, the look of derision,
that speaks of disgust; so what will you employ?

When meeting another, our look and our language
will speak of our love or our will to exclude;
the stranger is waiting, the door that we're keeping,
can open or close, it can bar or include.

So there in our neighbour is Christ that we damage,
is Christ we abuse by each word and each act;
is Christ that we welcome with loving expression,
is Christ who will judge not the mask but the fact.

Metre: 12.11.12.11.

Suggested Tune: STREETS OF LAREDO

In my better moments I'm aware that justice and judgement are not abstract or remote concepts. If you were to meet me you would be aware from my body language, the look on my face, what I am thinking of you – I don't think I'd be a very good poker player! In every human contact we make we affirm or deny, demonstrate understanding or condemnation. Rarely are our interactions neutral. This text was written in 2003 at Lake Junaluska at the Academy of Global Song run by the United Methodist Church Board of Global Ministries, after hearing Jorge Lockward speaking.

103   With no excess baggage, the Christ travelled light

With no excess baggage, the Christ travelled light;
while greed is our watchword, we grasp wealth as right.
No shelter, no riches, no place for a bed,
with frost as a blanket he laid down his head.

In touching, in meeting, in singing love's song,
we learn Christ's humility, seek to right wrong;
in rhythm, through dancing, we're travelling light,
we waltz from the darkness, we leap into light.

We each touch a hand as we pass through the dance.
In living love's rhythm we glimpse Jesus' glance.
We share in his story, we're travelling light,
we're living his love through each day and each night.

Metre: 11 11.11 11.

Suggested Tune: ST DENIO

The gospel tells us that the son of man had nowhere to rest his head. I need reminding constantly that possessions are unimportant. In a disconnected way this hymn began when the third verse was inspired by words of the eponymous TV detective Frost.

Imagination of the heart
will rise on soaring wings of song;
will elevate our bland desires,
transcend our human wrong.

The spirit will inspire, define
the love that gives this passage worth,
the pain we gather on the way,
the trust of love's new birth.

We emulate that wild design,
the flaunting serenade to peace
that brought a saviour to his knees
that brought a thief release.

High-handed love, incarnate hope,
that freed our stony hearts by grace;
we offer praise, it is your due,
from all the human race.

Metre: 8.8.8.6.

Suggested Tune: IMAGINATION OF THE HEART

At its best, Christian life mirrors exactly the life of Jesus. These words were written after reading an obituary of the poet Kathleen Raine (1908–2003).

IMAGINATION OF THE HEART

Peter Sharrocks (1940–)

I - ma - gi - na - tion of the heart_____ will rise on soar-ing wings of song; will e - le - vate our bland de - sires, tran-scend our hu - man wrong. The spi-rit will in-spire, de-fine the love that gives this pas-sage worth, the pain we ga - ther on the way, the trust of love's new birth.

Earth-maker, source of the world and our wisdom,
lover and carer, forever the same.
Bread for our sustenance, all we have needed,
you offer freely, we worship your name.

Pain-bearer, holding the fragile and faulted,
loving the broken and tending the frail;
bringing forgiveness and grace for our mending,
you are the heaven where love will not fail.

Life-giver, offering justice and mercy,
needing your presence we come at your call;
hallow your name through the whole of creation,
you reign in glory for ever and all!

Metre: 11.10.11.10.

Suggested Tunes: STEWARDSHIP and WAS LEBET

Jim Cotter's version of the 'Lord's Prayer' published in 'Prayer at Night' (Cairns Publications, 1988) inspired this hymn. The interpretation underlines for me a call to justice that is at the centre of the gospel – how can we pray 'Our Father' and 'Give us this day our daily bread' without committing ourselves to the equitable sharing of the gifts of creation?

In lives of justice

God is the grounding of all we accomplish,
source of all grace and the goal of all good;
seen in the person of Jesus, now human,
born in a stable then nailed to the wood.

Christ in the centre, still sharing our struggles,
enters each wound, offers balm to each pain;
holds, in our anguish, life nearly extinguished,
comforting, loving will always remain.

Spirit of God you have blown through your people,
charging, empowering with love and with grace.
Move us still further beyond this existence
till, in each neighbour, we meet face to face.

© Copyright 2006 Stainer & Bell Ltd

Metre: 11.10.11.10.

Suggested Tunes: WAS LEBET and QUEDLINBURG

My Christian pilgrimage has led me to understand that I am never likely to have a creed which, to quote Sydney Carter, is either fixed or final. Experience continually challenges our faith and changes our understanding of God. If I return to what is apparently an orthodox trinitarian interpretation it is because, in the context of what I am writing or saying, it makes sense to me. And so this text was written with the conviction that God is the ground of everything, that the nature of God is apparent in Christ, and that there is a spirit which, when we respond to it, can enable us to see that same God in each and every neighbour. When that happens we have achieved the greatest possible compulsion to living justly.

What is money? Source of greed?
Or a means of building wealth?
Tokens used to foster fear,
or to build a way to health?

Jesus granted we should give
what authorities command,
but that does not give us leave
to avoid love's quiet demand.

So we ought to give to God,
bind each bruised or broken reed,
offer back all we receive
as we meet our neighbour's need.

Metre: 7.7.7.7.

Suggested Tunes: VIENNA and SAVANNAH

'Take my silver and my gold' – words which spring to mind when we think of hymns and money. After a fruitless search at Bispham Methodist Church for a contemporary hymn on this theme I wrote these words.

In searching for a way to love
we're countered by humanity
that turns our loving upside down
and makes us what we would not be.

How can we find a way beyond
this paradox, that holds and binds
emasculating good intent,
that grapples with our hearts and minds?

God, show us how to love again
with free, unfettered selflessness,
until your fire of love consumes
those things that fuel our selfishness.

Help us to lose ourselves in you
conceived in every neighbour's need:
until our cup of life is full
and all are filled and all are freed.

Metre: LM

Suggested Tune: BRESLAU

For years I have been aware for myself of the truth of the words of St Paul: 'For I do not do the good I want, but the evil I do not want is what I do.' (Romans 7:19, NRSV). The words speak, I believe, of a universal experience. And again, trying to make sense of theology, of scripture, I struggle with verse.

In lives that mirror back the love
incarnate through a birth
that led, through turmoil, to a cross,
we show another's worth.

To tread the path that Jesus trod,
to wear compassion's face,
we need to lose the love of self
and trust the power of grace.

The free, unfettered love of God,
this way, this truth, this life,
can overcome our human fear
and drown our needless strife.

Then let us share this holy love
until our loving's spent,
until the world suffused with joy
responds to God's intent.

Metre: CM

Suggested Tune: BELMONT

Jesus is a window into God. In Jesus's way of life I see the life I'd like to live. I also see the life which demonstrates what heights human life can achieve when lived for the other to the uttermost. I fail, but I want to continue trying.

We are lords of all creation
with the power to break or mend;
playing 'god' we tune the genome
from life's birthing to its end.

We are stewards, but forgetful
of responsibility
to the gift you give to nurture:
cosmic creativity.

God, forgive our selfish grasping,
calling what you loan our own.
We rejoice in your creation;
help us share all you have sown.

Help us work with your direction,
taking joy in all you give.
Let us join as co-creators,
spirit, hone the lives we live.

Metre: 8.7.8.7.

Suggested Tune: ALL FOR JESUS

The further we progress humanly, scientifically, the easier it is to think that we can 'play god'. Many years ago I was on track to do a PhD in fish pharmacology. I achieved a Masters, but then pulled out on ethical grounds. Perhaps because of this I have a continuing fascination with scientific progress and the ethics associated with it.

Thrown out by God to all the world,
to go we know not where;
we walk in faith, our certainty:
we know God will be there.

Beyond the earthquake, wind and fire,
through every flood or storm,
consistent grace has gone before;
we sense this is the norm.

And so we humbly hear the word,
we celebrate its worth,
then, driven by the spirit's power,
we'll go to all the earth.

Metre: CM

Suggested Tune: AMAZING GRACE

When I began to study theology I was led to read St Mark's Gospel in Greek. I am no Greek scholar, but I was and am impressed by the energy, almost the coarseness of Mark's language and expression, the pace of the narrative. As Mark speaks of Jesus going into the wilderness after his baptism the word he uses is that of Jesus being impelled to go, better, hurled into the desert ('And the Spirit immediately drove him out into the wilderness.' Mark 1:12, NRSV). So, when we think of the way in which we go to witness, is it any wonder that sometimes we feel a sudden dislocation and that our landing is not always comfortable? This hymn was written after listening to Martyn Atkins speaking about Cliff College, where he is the Principal.

The word, its essence, breathes through all creation
for us to nurture, recognise and hear;
for all this sound has offered revelation
for saint and prophet, follower and seer.

The energy and matter from formation
that permeate the cosmic reach of space,
still energise our thought and contemplation,
will meet each human life with sudden grace.

And so to all the people who would follow,
God utters wisdom as they proffer praise;
the love that weaves between each joy and sorrow
is constant at all times and through all days.

Metre: 11.10.11.10.

Suggested Tune: INTERCESSOR

I have been fascinated by the image of the Logos in St John's Gospel. The idea is conveyed of an essence of creation that was the ground of all things that exist. In scientific, cosmic terms my mind imagines this essence being the source of the origin of the cosmos. For me this gospel is excitingly scientific. The opening chapter argues that this essence was human in Jesus. I would argue that the presence of the spirit in and through God's people is that same Logos. We are grounded in and inspired by that which formed the cosmos. Again, I try to make sense of this in verse.

God comes in unexpected ways
to interrupt our fast:
the needy face, the unseen hand
bring love to grow and last.

Such faces go unrecognised.
The Christ we fail to see
is hidden in a shifting crowd
of lost humanity.

The words we speak are platitudes,
an empty, hollow creed,
until we risk, hold out our hand,
and sense our neighbour's need.

Metre: CM

Suggested Tune: ST PETER (Reinagle)

Catherine de Hueck Doherty wrote a book entitled 'Poustinia: Encountering God in Silence, Solitude and Prayer' (revised edition, Madonna House, 2000). I came across this book many years ago, but one theme in it has stayed with me. In the book she speaks of the Poustinik, the hermit, who lives outside the village in a house which, metaphorically, has three walls. The hermit, while living alone, is always open to the calls and needs of the community who may interrupt at any time. Such interruptions are seen as of God. I find the image compelling and, particularly when people interrupt me, challenging!

Grace for the few is not our claim,
but grace for every race and time;
love for the world we will proclaim
through every latitude or clime.

Sing of the love that God inspires,
sing of the word, the source of all,
sing of the spirit's driving force,
as, faithfully, we heed God's call.

Now we will go to love the world,
none are excluded on God's earth,
whatever name or creed you claim,
we share a common ground and birth.

Give me your hand, let's live in peace
through sharing, learning, love and faith;
each called by God, God's family,
we'll live as one through time and space.

Metre: LM

Suggested Tunes: EISENACH and WAREHAM

As we move into the world we need to know to whom we are going. I am a Methodist by choice. A central tenet of my denomination is Arminianism. In brief this is the understanding that no one is outside the scope of God's grace. Charles Wesley took this as his theme in many hymns. I wanted to experiment with a hymn which would affirm that same belief today. The result has a slightly 'old' feel to it, I think. It stands here as evidence of the rootedness of my faith in the tradition in which I stand.

115   How immense your faith must be

How immense your faith must be,
putting children in our hands.
Wonderful – the love you give;
trusting us with their demands.

Children who will change and grow,
nurture life and cherish grace,
move with strength beyond our time,
cope with shifting change and pace.

Keep us faithful for their care,
let us watch them grow and move;
grasp the wisdom that they share,
make us worthy of such love.

Metre: 7.7.7.7.

Suggested Tune: MONKLAND

Watching my great nieces and nephew, Melody, Madeleine and Isaac, I have been amazed that we should be given the responsibility for the growth and nurture of children. We sing 'Great is thy faithfulness', and this for me is a sign of the faith that God places in us. I envisage the hymn I have written being used for services of infant baptism or of dedication.

Going into all the world

The children would follow the peal of your piping,
the ring of your reason, the joy of your love,
the children would follow, and none would deter them
from plateaus so barren to mountains above.

And those who are childlike still follow your calling;
a calling to suffer, yet dusted with hope.
The way to fulfilment, to peace and to plenty,
is fissured and rutted but still we will cope.

God's joy is the centre of all that we hope for,
a calling for everyone, not just for some;
the music is moving, can't stop ourselves singing,
still Jesus is piping and still people come!

Metre: 12.11.12.11.

Suggested Tune: STREETS OF LAREDO

The story of the Pied Piper is fascinating. For some reason I was playing around in my mind with the verses from St Luke's Gospel: 'They are like children sitting in the market-place and calling to one another, "We played the flute for you, and you did not dance; we wailed, and you did not weep."' (Luke 7:32, NRSV). The thoughts wound round each other and this text was the result. Again, the call is universal.

117 Whatever your race, your colour or creed

WHATEVER YOUR RACE

Alex Jarrett (1980–)

What-e-ver your race, your co-lour or creed you are a sis-ter or bro-ther to me. You speak with a lan-guage I don't un-der-stand but I want to learn what you mean.

So

FINE

Going into all the world

much we could share_ if you lis-ten to me,_ so much if I lis-ten to you.

Wher-e-ver you're from,_ and what-e-ver your need,_ how-

-e-ver you name_God, what-e-ver you plead,_ your cul-ture is fo-reign, un-u-

-sual to me_ but both of us want_ to be free._ *What-e-ver your*

Whatever your race, your colour or creed
you are a sister or brother to me.
You speak with a language I don't understand
but I want to learn what you mean.

Continued overleaf

So much we could share if you listen to me,
so much if I listen to you.
Wherever you're from, and whatever your need,
however you name God, whatever you plead,
your culture is foreign, unusual to me
but both of us want to be free.
Chorus

So much we could share if you listen to me,
so much if I listen to you.
When tragedy strikes and our lives spin around,
while babies are crying and battle resounds
I know you still love me, and I still love you,
I'll help with what you need to do.
Chorus

So much we could share if you listen to me,
so much if I listen to you.
So let's join together, the table is set,
the laughter and pleasure will help us forget
the fear at the difference that keeps us apart.
In loving we'll make a new start.
Chorus

Metre: 11.8.11 11.11 8. and Chorus 10.10.11.8.

Suggested Tune: WHATEVER YOUR RACE

In 2002 the Orrell and Lamberhead Green Circuit of the UK Methodist Church produced a musical, 'In at the Deep End', while I was minister there. This is one song from the musical. It is best sung by two people in dialogue with the congregation joining in for the chorus.

We look at people all around,
our friends from many nations;
some hardly known to us at all,
some known for generations.

The love of God, the bond that binds
us close to one another,
will help us face whatever comes
as sister and as brother.

We do not know what lies ahead
through war or devastation,
we only know what holds our lives,
spans ours and every nation.

Your love is stronger than the fear
that sows the seeds of hatred;
a love that we will keep alive
when all else has abated.

Metre: 8.7.8.7.

Suggested Tunes: DOMINUS REGIT ME and ST COLUMBA (Anonymous Irish)

My wife Jackie and I had been visiting a playground in Leyton in east London with Melody, my great niece. This place is popular with children and parents from Pakistan, Turkey, Italy, South America and Eastern Europe as well as England. On returning Melody to her mother we heard that United Nations personnel were being moved out of Iraq and that war was anticipated, which prompted this text.

Echoes of the organ's thunder
hang expectant, poignant, clear.
Filled with pregnant expectation
voices chorus: 'God is here'.
Alleluia! Alleluia! Alleluia!
Voices chorus: 'God is here'.

God is in our jubilation,
in the pain of damaged hope;
God surrounds with love, enfolds us,
giving strength and grace to cope.
Alleluia! Alleluia! Alleluia!
Give us strength and grace to cope.

God is present, God is waiting,
God will counter our despair.
Let the organ's mighty thunder
fade to silent, ceaseless prayer.
Alleluia! Alleluia! Alleluia!
Join the saints in ceaseless prayer.

Metre: 8.7.8.7.4.7.

Suggested Tunes: HELMSLEY

In my previous collection, 'Whatever Name or Creed', I included the text 'In darkness we traverse the rock', with the following words: 'Where is the faith that, mixed with doubt, / can underpin foundations, / that forms the footings that will stand / our grief's adjudications?' It is an echo of William Cowper's cry, 'Where is the blessedness I knew / when first I saw the Lord?' ('O for a closer walk with God'). After the death of my son I knew things would never be the same again. I don't think I even hoped for happiness, and as to praising God … Yet I suppose I nonetheless harboured a hope that one day I might at least be able to be positive, somehow to 'reclaim praise'. It has been a long journey to reach this point, yet there has been no denial of love or grief. And so I want next to share something of that longing pilgrimage. This text was written as an expression of hope rather than a reflection on reality 'on the way' to fulfilling Carson Cooman's request for a single-stanza 'invocation':

Let the organ thunder, let the building quake.
Filled with awe and wonder, let the people wake.
Fling the door wide open, welcome rich and poor,
through our praise and worship let us love, adore.

Children stagger into language,
trying to be understood,
so our faltering acclamations
speak to God of babyhood.

Any language that we borrow,
any words that we create,
fall as echoes, never framing
glory we anticipate.

In humility and silence
we must learn to wait and pray,
knowing language is imperfect,
in its time will pass away.

Only love can give expression,
silent love will hold and live,
God is love and love is lasting,
love received, that we may give.

Metre: 8.7.8.7.

Suggested Tunes: ST OSWALD and FOR THE BREAD

Finding faith or learning to cope with faith in new circumstances can be like a child learning a language. Sounds roll uncomfortably around our mouths and don't always come out as we want or expect them to. As my great niece, Melody, learned to speak she mimicked us but also framed her own sounds and words in order to communicate. It struck me that when we enter into theological or doxological discourse before God we are like babies. Ultimately, love is the language that enables our 'God-talk'. But we are always learning.

Why should I praise this living God,
or love my neighbour as myself?
Expedience claims my innocence,
my cynicism cries for self.

Yet God has brought me to this point
and now, within this place and time,
I need to find a way ahead
that seasons life, that offers rhyme;

that flavours existential things,
that gives a savour to this day,
that helps transcend this time and place,
and opens up another way.

Let love be found and peace be born,
let stress be banished as you lead
my life beside the quiet streams,
God be my shepherd, care and feed.

God fill my life with selflessness,
that I might realise the dream,
the vision you have given me,
and find my place within your scheme.

Metre: LM

Suggested Tune: WHY JOIN A LARGE AND NOISY CROWD?

In the depths of hurt or despair there can sometimes seem to be no reason for praise or gratitude. Even then a small seed of hope can remain.

WHY JOIN A LARGE AND NOISY CROWD?

George F. Bexon (1958–)

Why should I praise this liv-ing God, or love my neigh-bour as my-

-self? Ex-pe-dience claims my in-no-cence, my cy-ni-ci-sm cries for

self? Yet God has brought me to this point and now, with-in this place and

time, I need to find a way a-head that seas-ons life, that of-fers

rhyme; that fla-vours ex-ist-en-tial me, and find my place with-in your scheme.

Repeat twice, the second time, for verse 5, ending halfway through and going to the end.

© Copyright 1999 Stainer & Bell Ltd

Longing to praise again

Take a tune, make mysteries friendly,
play the music of your heart,
reach within each treasured memory,
cultivate your precious art.

All your saying, feeling, seeing,
all your history, where you home,
make a context for your singing,
give a sense of what you own.

Never lose your rich tradition,
never lose your sense of place,
yet, this is no contradiction,
find new signs of love and grace.

In the essence of your music,
Christ, the starting point of song,
brings new fragrance to each meeting,
helps us all to love along.

Metre: 8.7.8.7.

Suggested Tune: STUTTGART

Sometimes I find that memories from my childhood have provided comfort. When Carlton Young, quoting Erik Routley, spoke in a lecture of 'making mysteries friendly' a whole chain of thoughts went racing across the page.

How do we worship in a world
distrusting wonder, love and awe,
where people live their lives alone
where reason rules and doubts can soar?

How can we open eyes to God
so blinded by a cosmic fear?
How can we bring the Christ alive
in love both tangible and near?

Christ is embodied in our lives.
Love must inspire another phase;
living the gospel that we preach,
finding, in people, cause to praise!

Metre: LM

Suggested Tunes: NIAGARA and CORNISH

The world in which we live is more resistant to awe, perhaps, than once it was. We are less easily shocked or impressed. Yet awe is an intrinsic part of the relationship we have with God. How can we gain this sense today if our lives are lived in the bustle of the city, while the seas, mountains, lakes and forests are distant, only accessible through our television screens?

Where is the evidence of love,
God's presence in our days?
What is the reason for our faith,
the motive for our praise?

Here in the fellowship we find
the comfort of God's grace.
Here in the presence of a friend
the essence of love's face.

But is there hope, or only hell
within the world today?
And can we sing in songs of joy
or bend our heads to pray?

Here is the reason to believe
that love is dancing on,
for when we feel the touch of love
all sense of doubt is gone.

Metre: CM

Suggested Tunes: FINGAL and FORGIVE OUR SINS (DETROIT)

As we begin to regain the capacity to praise, doubts can sometimes raise their heads again. For me, tangible things counter doubt, or at least make belief more reasonable.

Here and now our faith is growing,
God pours blessings on our lives.
In the midst of joy or sorrow,
God is present, love survives.

Here and now we come together
seeking peace by quiet lakes,
God is present in this meeting,
mends each spirit when it breaks.

Here and now we meet together,
meet for praise and meet for prayer;
meet to further understanding
of the grace and faith we share.

Here and now when bread is broken,
when a hungry child is fed,
as we give ourselves to others,
we will follow where Christ led.

Here and now we find a purpose,
find a reason for our lives,
in our living, striving, caring,
alleluia! love survives!

Metre: 8.7.8.7.

Suggested Tunes: SHIPSTON and GALILEE (Jude)

As I explored worship and found my way back, I continued to express myself through hymnody. This text was written in the Liverpool Methodist District Synod for Bispham Methodist Church's weekend in Coniston, 2003. The second verse may be altered to: 'Here and now in city centres / busy towns, by quiet lakes, / God is present in each meeting, / mends each spirit when it breaks.'

What on earth is life about,
this laughter, love and living?
A time for us to pray, to praise,
a time for selfless giving?
Bread is baking, bread is broken,
yet our love lies battered,
hungry people grasp for food
where dusty crumbs are scattered.

Where on earth can God be found
as traffic drowns our singing?
Throughout the world, across the street,
a quiet voice is ringing.
Hearts are breaking, tears are falling,
counters to our wonder.
Awe is less to do with God
than callous bombers' thunder.

So we go to all the world,
a rising, praising people,
we're not content to be confined
by liturgy or steeple.
God is calling, we're responding,
lives are for the giving,
stepping out we trust God's grace,
our lives are for the living.

Metre: 7.7.8.7.8.6.7.7.

Suggested Tune: LIFE SONG

At last I began to find a new sense of purpose. A range of circumstances gave rise to this, and I am beginning to trace God's presence in and through this renewal. It is not that the questions had gone or that the pain of grief was any less. Moving from the area where I had been ministering when my son was killed was a start, though this text came much later, in 2006, as I returned to the Liverpool Methodist District for a celebration day.

June Baker (1936–)

What on earth is life a-bout, this laugh-ter, love and liv - ing? A

time for us to pray, to praise, a time for self - less giv - ing?

Bread is bak - ing, bread is brok - en, yet our love lies bat - tered,

hun-gry peo - ple grasp for food where dust - y crumbs are scat - tered.

Rejoicing in praise reclaimed

When we can sense God's glory
incarnate in our midst,
with clouds of grace descending,
and love like morning mist,
then wonder is awakened
and awe is not dismissed.

The quality of silence,
the rising of the sun;
an air of expectation:
behold, the three in one!
Our worship has not ended;
all praise, it's just begun!

Melodic strains are rising
from voices, not yet known.
We join with them in chorus,
no longer sing alone.
We share a mightier music,
a pure angelic tone.

All praise to God our parent:
proud alleluias bring!
All praise to God the Christ child:
loud alleluias sing!
All praise to God the spirit:
let alleluias ring!

Metre: 7.6.7.6.7.6.

Suggested Tune: INCARNATE GLORY

This hymn was written during and after a Liverpool area meeting of the Royal School of Church Music on 3 July 2003. 'Mightier music' quotes the title of a book about the 'Methodist Hymn Book' of 1933.

Ian Sharp (1943–)

When we can sense God's glo-ry_____ in - car - nate in___ our midst,___ with

clouds of grace de-scend-ing,_____ and love like morn - ing mist,_____ then

Verse 4 optional descant

let al — le — lu - ias ring!

won - der is___ a - wa - kened and awe____ is___ not___ dis-missed.

This place of sweet solemnity,
is shafted through with shouts of praise,
love bids us welcome, not draw back,
on this God's day of days.

This place of humble charity,
where none will ever be despised,
is where malignant hurt is healed,
simplicity is prized.

This place where we may rest and stay,
a sanctuary of hope at night,
is where we come with confidence
to praise God's love and light.

Metre: 8.8.8.6.

Suggested Tune: MISERICORDIA (Smart)

We are at our best when we judge charitably and hopefully the place where we worship, the community with which we share. It is not that we should be uncritical, but looking positively at anything is far more creative than looking negatively. John Wesley once went 'very unwillingly' to a meeting. However unwilling I sometimes feel, I want to hold on to a grain of expectation. This hymn is written from such a perspective, and even if it does not mirror our experience, perhaps it might remind us of what we might be and how our churches could be.

God is love, love born among us;
utmost love has framed our creed;
and that love will look and suffer,
fashioning grace to meet our need.

God is love, that love enlivens
where we stand and where we walk;
love the constant inspiration
fires our argument and talk.

God is love, participating
in creation on this earth;
love that circumscribes the cosmos,
bringing worlds and stars to birth.

God is love, the ground of being,
God is love, the final goal;
love, the final consummation,
born through love, through love made whole.

Metre: 8.7.8.7.

Suggested Tunes: STAPLEGROVE and CHARLESTOWN

Years ago I was criticised for having only one theme for my sermons – 'God is love'. A lot of things have changed, but that theme remains central to my belief.

What wonders shine through glistening dew,
or in the cataclysmic shower,
that put a cosmic drama on the stage,
unleashed its love and power.

And God is in and through this scene,
a woven narrative of grace,
held taut between this time and every age,
and wears a human face.

Our hope is here in open hands
pierced through with nails, held bound, yet free.
See! All the glories of our hope, these palms,
that hold a world, and me.

Metre: 8.8.10.6.

Suggested Tune: GLISTENING DEW

The love for which we hope, in which we believe, can be reborn, can be found again even after the most horrendous events and sometimes in the midst of them. Often it is found in those around us. This hymn was written during Professor Vincent Newey's lecture entitled 'The Olney Hymns', given at the 2002 conference of the Hymn Society of Great Britain and Ireland, held at Leicester.

GLISTENING DEW

Peter Sharrocks (1940–)

What won-ders shine through gli-sten-ing___ dew, ___ or in the ca-ta-clys-mic sho-wer, that put a cos-mic dra-ma on the stage, un-leashed its love and pow-er.___

In love reborn

The love of Christ is greater
than any human loss,
as God confronts extinction
by crippling on the cross.

Where shallow love would falter,
the love of Christ prevails:
for grace is not extinguished
by piercing of the nails.

He uttered, 'It is finished,'
as human life expired,
and in that dereliction
the force of love was fired.

The kindled flame went blazing
beyond all space and time,
the end of all creation
found incandescent rhyme.

The spirit is a signal
that love is still aflame,
a present incarnation
not held within a frame.

Metre: 7.6.7.6.

Suggested Tune: HAMBRIDGE

Many people have a favourite Bible text, and mine is: 'For I am convinced that neither death, nor life, nor angels, nor rulers, nor things present, nor things to come, nor powers, nor height, nor depth, nor anything else in all creation, will be able to separate us from the love of God in Christ Jesus our Lord.' (Romans 8:38–39, NRSV). I return to these words again and again. Sometimes they make more sense than at other times.

Joyful songs of broken people,
smiling faces, lilting praise,
welcome those who come to worship
in the cauldron of these days.

Listen to this fragile story,
born in poverty and fear,
thousands, now ten thousand voices,
ringing out that God is near.

Near, because we carry with us
love that counters every smart,
love that holds, that binds, protects us,
love of God in every heart.

Metre: 8.7.8.7.

Suggested Tune: DRAKES BROUGHTON

When our faith is strong we can challenge God if we feel forsaken, and we can encourage one another. That is not a blind, insensitive encouragement that says everything is alright when it isn't. It is an encouragement saying that though we are broken we hold each other, that we will never stop holding on to hope. Peter Storey preached and wrote to challenge the iniquity of apartheid, and his words from 'With God in the Crucible: Preaching Costly Discipleship' (Abingdon Press, 2002) inspired this hymn.

Mighty force that formed the cosmos,
ground of being, time and space,
God of eloquence we praise you
for transcendent, boundless grace.

Grace incarnate, born among us,
Christ the window to your love,
human challenge to our living,
fleshed on earth, not hid above.

Spirit, bring your ringing presence
to this moment, to this hour.
As we bow in prayer before you,
bring your Pentecostal power.

Metre: 8.7.8.7.

Suggested Tunes: WYCHBOLD and RATHBUN

The source of our hope is the ground of all that exists, greater than all that is or is to be. I return again to wonder and awe, engendered by my view of the cosmos and by amazement that Jesus is a window into this ground of being.

Spilling sunshine, love and laughter,
Christ will live, death can't destroy.
On the resurrection morning
all the world will dance with joy.

Symbols sign our exaltation,
crosses decked with springtime flowers,
wine is drunk and bread is broken,
all the grace of God is ours.

Join the throng and sing God's praises,
alleluias ring the earth!
Alleluia! Praise the Godhead,
source of love and hope's rebirth.

Metre: 8.7.8.7.

Suggested Tunes: SHIPSTON and WELLESLEY (Tourjee)

The times at which we realise things about our faith, the times at which our faith deepens, are not set to church calendars or the times of the year. Just before Christmas in 2004 I wrote a few hymns relating to resurrection. Most unseasonable! But for me this was a time of renewal, so somehow the hymns made sense to my religious psyche! The words came, the texts were written. Some churches where I have ministered have adopted the practice of erecting a large cross outside on Good Friday, and decking it with flowers on Easter Sunday to symbolise resurrection.

Strong shoulders of a loving God,
you lift your children up;
you carry us through fear and storm,
you are both food and cup.

Kind features of a caring God,
your loving knows no bounds;
you welcome those who turn to you,
hear how our praise resounds!

Calm spirit of a quiet God,
you give to us your rest,
a peace we cannot comprehend,
in all we have the best.

Metre: CM

Suggested Tunes: WETHERBY and LAND OF REST (Anonymous American)

Resurrection gives rise to praise, and so can reflecting on God's care and God's providence. My great niece loved being carried on my shoulders. This led me to reflect on the way God 'carries' us. My thought then moved to the parable of the Prodigal Son and the way in which a father greets him on his return. Lastly, I moved to the idea of the 'peace which passes understanding'.

In creative loving, searching,
words are spoken, feelings aired,
sense and thought revealed and honoured.
Is this loving mutual, shared?
Past the drama of decision,
now they know that love is real.
Language cannot give expression
to the joy this couple feel.

Now in company they're standing.
God is present in our midst,
and the covenant we witness
they will seal with ring and kiss.
Most profound imagination
cannot frame the joy they know,
and our prayers are offered for them
that their love may thrive and grow.

As we laugh and feast together,
may this day of joy sustain
these two lovers in their loving,
and in times of stress or pain.
Present when they found each other,
mirrored in the love they share,
God enfold them with your blessing,
deepen joy and strengthen care.

Metre: 8.7.8.7.D.

Suggested Tune: HYFRYDOL

When a couple marry they give expression to a love they have found, which has been born between them, which has been nurtured and has grown. And sometimes, in the energy of the moment, old loves are rekindled and reborn as well. These words were offered to Elizabeth my niece and her fiancé Nicholas, as they prepared for marriage.

This is our mother, the source of all being,
sharpening starlight, then raising the dawn,
singing forth sunshine, then playing with laughter,
scattering teardrops, in passion newborn.

Mother of oceans, so careful with splendour,
ground of creation and centre of life,
love in abundance, all caring, all seeing,
counter to conflict, now staying our strife.

This is our mother, the God of our parents,
source of the hope that has brought them to be,
present to hold us, then leading us onward,
loving, renewing, and setting us free.

Metre: 11.10.11.10.

Suggested Tunes: EPIPHANY HYMN and WAS LEBET

As we find love renewed, so we can rediscover hope. The image of God as mother is again, for me, helpful in this context.

When in the depths we kneel and pray,
in penitence for all that's past,
an honest prayer wrung from the heart,
then praise is pure, and praise will last.

When from our work we turn to prayer
and seeking God in silent fast,
then deep within this quiet art
our praise is pure, our praise will last.

When in our worship, from our prayer,
new hopes and dreams are born and cast
into the world, beyond the church,
our praise is pure, our praise will last.

Metre: LM

Suggested Tune: AGINCOURT (DEO GRACIAS)

In Cape Coast slaves were kept downstairs while divine worship took place upstairs. The hypocrisy is clear to us now. It was not clear to the church then. As I write these notes, there are preparations taking place in the UK to recognise the place that slavery has had in building the wealth of this nation. And we are called to repent. Though praise is pure when it begins in penitence, it must not end there, but must reach into the world, affecting our actions, our commerce, our politics, and our lives. Then we become agents of hope. These words were written at the 2003 conference of the Hymn Society of Great Britain and Ireland, held in Canterbury.

From mundane tasks we step across
a threshold to the holy;
anticipate rich gain, not loss,
yet find that we are lowly.

The awe, the wonder that we greet,
defies imagination.
We fall before God's mercy seat
in hopeful expectation.

The love of God has drawn us near;
we need the intervention
of grace to dissipate our fear,
to culture re-creation.

And life is fresh, yes, life is new,
and praise renews our journey.
The road is long, but cares are few,
Christ's spirit, our attorney.

God reaches through each fault and sin
a hand to calm our crying,
and now we're free and we begin
to live in spite of dying.

Metre: 8.7.8.7.

Suggested Tunes: ACH GOTT UND HERR and ST COLUMBA (Anonymous Irish)

There is an understanding that when we enter worship, wherever that may be, we cross a threshold to holy ground. This is the place of change, the crucible where love is forged, the context where we can find resurrection now.

Rhythmic, mothering, holy spirit,
childhood voice we understand;
love's cascade, we're bathed within it,
tide of love that warms the strand.

Homely sense of God around us,
light in darkness, joy in play;
so secure for God has found us,
fire by night and cloud by day.

As we grow and leave the safety
of the home that we know best,
life's sharp flavours turn more tasty,
freedom gives a greater test.

Sometimes we feel lost, forsaken,
sometimes filled with holy joy,
each sensation will awaken
love that nothing can destroy.

Babbling, bubbling, foaming spirit,
lead us onward to the height,
then confirm, and let us sense it:
God is ours and love beams bright.

Metre: 8.7.8.7.

Suggested Tunes: ST CATHERINE (Jones) and CHARLESTOWN

Faith may grow in fits and starts, setbacks and revivals. This has been my experience. And yet, looking at my life in retrospect, I have a sense that all the while God has been there, though how I have described that God and the way I have named that God have changed with my understanding.

Fighting the ocean, and losing,
seeking the shore of your love,
rolling and tossing and reeling,
spun by the wind from above.

Spirit, you found me and held me,
saved me to walk in your way,
steadied my feet then you lifted,
taught me to dance and to pray.

Here where your messenger sought me,
life was mismatched and abused.
Here, through your grace you have raised me,
now I'm no longer confused.

Now I'm at one with creation,
God, you have brought me release,
here you have set me in beauty,
caught me and brought me to peace.

Metre: 8.7.8.7.

Suggested Tune: OCEAN SONG

Sometimes, holding on to faith in times of change or renewal is not easy. John Wesley famously described how his heart had been 'strangely warmed' after his experience of conversion. But he also reflected on how the sense of elation he had seen in others had been withheld from him. The presence of God was real enough, motivating him to change the direction of his life, to re-evaluate his place before God. Yet he was doubtful, asking himself, 'This cannot be faith; for where is thy joy?' Let us hope that we will pass through uncertainty to something more sure.

OCEAN SONG

Peter Sharrocks (1940–)

Fight-ing the o - cean, and los - ing, seek-ing the shore of your love, roll-ing and toss - ing and reel - ing, spun by the wind from a - bove.

Here where your mes - sen - ger sought me, life was mis-matched and a - bused. Here, through your grace— you have raised me, now I'm no long - er con - fused.

In hope rekindled

We're dancing through salvation,
not straggling from the past,
not a pathetic remnant,
we sing of love that lasts.
Within the fiery furnace
of persecution's pain,
we stand for peace and justice,
trust love will live again.

God's grace our vindication,
foundation of our hope,
that painful consecration
can elevate our scope.
We look beyond the present,
we live above the past,
we celebrate the future
assured that love will last.

Metre: 7.6.7.6.D.

Suggested Tunes: THORNBURY and BRED DINA VIDA VINGAR

The sense of hope that God engenders is not just individual, as a collection of addresses and sermons given by a white Methodist minister in South Africa during the apartheid era demonstrates. 'We are not some pathetic remnant trying vainly to recall a lost past; we are heralds of God's new future!' (Peter Storey, 'With God in the Crucible: Preaching Costly Discipleship' (Abingdon Press, 2002), page 67).

Brightly

We're dancing through sal - va - tion, not strag - gling from the past, not a pa - the - tic rem - nant, we sing of love that lasts.

Optional descant for verse 2

With - in the fie - ry fur - nace of per - se - cu - tion's pain, we stand for peace and jus - tice, trust love will live a - gain.

In hope rekindled

143   Another year is past, what lies ahead?

Another year is past, what lies ahead?
We never know, the future is untold;
but with God's grace we enter it in faith,
the years may turn but love will not grow old.

The days roll on, and nature's colours change,
the seasons move through winter, spring and fall;
the summer of our life is sometimes chilled,
but God will journey with us through it all.

So let us sing and celebrate this day
with all who share what we proclaim with joy,
that God has seen us through with boundless love
that nothing can diminish or destroy.

© Copyright 2006 Stainer & Bell Ltd

Metre: 10.10.10.10.

Suggested Tune: WOODLANDS

At our best we feel a sense of security and safety within God's care. We feel close to and at one with God, and experience a sense of serenity. How we describe this feeling varies, and it is a feeling that may come and go. There are times when we feel safer than at others. But when we do have this assurance it is worth celebrating, and it is worth putting down a marker in some way to remind us of its reality when life is not so good. These words were written for the birthday of Ray Makeever, an American religious singer–songwriter and pastor. They were used at Clowes Methodist Church watchnight service on 31 December 2003 and at Bispham and Orrell covenant services in January 2004. In the first line 'year' can be replaced with 'phase'.

Secure in the love of God

144 As life unfolds, each day, each hour

As life unfolds, each day, each hour,
from rising sun and early morn,
our God is here, will never leave,
will hold us safe through fear or storm.

Across the fields to mountain heights,
on sullen streets, in city grime,
in richness or in poverty,
God enters every space and time.

As day moves on, through quiet or din,
in life, in love, in pain, through death,
we walk, we work, in strain or stress,
God lives and shares our every breath.

The darkness comes, we glimpse the stars.
The earth revolves as others keep
their waking watch, we take our rest.
Good shepherd guard us while we sleep.

Metre: LM

Suggested Tunes: WINCHESTER NEW and WOODWORTH

*We need to go on reminding ourselves that God who watches over us 'neither slumbers nor sleeps'
(Psalm 121).*

Where art and life merge seamlessly,
where love and song are one,
here God with joy moves ceaselessly,
and heaven has begun.

Prepare your eyes to see the gold,
to cross the crystal sea,
to join with martyrs young and old,
and know that you are free.

Yes, free to sing and bid to dance
with angels round God's throne:
these metaphors inform the trance,
the vision that we own.

While on a lower plain we dwell
our song will never end,
and God will evermore excel:
our hope, our dream, our end!

Metre: CM

Suggested Tune: BISHOPTHORPE

Sometimes when reflecting on the 'good times', I wonder whether they might be a taste of heaven. Even if this taste is half as good as the reality, I can't wait. But that is suggesting that heaven is out there, somewhere beyond where we are now. Could it be that these times of exaltation are heaven itself? Or is this a delusion? I only know that the good times are very good and I thank God for them!

When God's spirit lends a lightness
to the songs we want to sing,
when we celebrate the brightness
that the love of God can bring;
then the grace of God surprises,
and our faith in God grows strong,
as the praise that we have sought for
is re-echoed in our song.

Here in song we find a freedom,
music wings our words on high,
now we know this is the season,
now we know the reason why
life is filled with exaltation,
joy inspires each love and life,
lifts beyond our expectation,
brings an end to former strife.

On beyond our pain and sorrow,
walking onward into light,
we will greet a new tomorrow
colours flaming out of night.
Light is dawning on the future,
guiding us within this maze;
love and grace will hold and nurture,
forming faith, reclaiming praise.

Metre: 8.7.8.7.D.

Suggested Tune: ABBOT'S LEIGH

God is always, it seems to me, offering new beginnings. This text was written with the idea that God's grace can enable us to reclaim praise when we thought it was an impossibility. Such a discovery always brings surprise.

The cosmos is revolving with endless rhythmic rhyme,
the circle keeps on turning to mark off chance and time;
and through the life we're living and images we see
we plot the hopeful story of God's eternity.

The summer sheds its harvest as autumn turns to gold,
the springtime and its newness are lost in time, grown old;
the cold of winter beckons, the trees are crippled, bare,
but seeds of hope are hidden, await the spring's repair.

This broadens expectation, the life for which we hope,
the gift of resurrection, the faith for which we grope,
are found within our compass and not beyond our grasp,
these gifts of grace and loving are sown in us to last.

Metre: 13 13.13 13.

Suggested Tune: SPROWSTON

This text is dedicated to the memory of Sydney Carter, who lives on in his words and music.

SPROWSTON

Basil E. Bridge (1927–)

The cos-mos is____ re - volv - ing with end-less rhyth-mic rhyme,
the cir - cle keeps_ on__ turn - ing to mark off chance and time;

and_through the life_ we're liv - ing and i - ma - ges_ we_ see we

plot the hope - ful__ stor - y of God's et - er - ni - ty.

Secure in the love of God

Soaring with the wings of eagles
to a realm of burnished light,
we will wing beyond conception,
far beyond the seraph's flight.

We will find our way to heaven,
though our reason loses rhyme,
here by love's divine intention,
drawn beyond this space and time.

Indestructible in spirit,
we were made by love's own sigh,
now imagination's glory
offers praise and we reply.

Metre: 8.7.8.7.

Suggested Tunes: ADORATION (Hunt) and SUNSET (Stebbins)

Religions through the ages have tried to understand the world and the place of humanity within it. They have sought to look beyond death, the inevitable termination of our lives, to hope for something more. These words were written after watching a television programme about the construction of the pyramids.

Source of sustenance, we savour
all the fruits sown by your grace,
and we relish every flavour,
such abundance, every trace.

God you are the sole life-giver,
all creation bears your mark,
cosmic history tells your story,
born through every flame and spark.

As we chronicle achievement,
contemplate the present day,
this is not the end, your zenith
dwells beyond our human stay.

You transcend the life before us,
where imagination quails,
limitless beyond extinction,
treasured love that never fails.

Metre: 8.7.8.7.

Suggested Tunes: ST OSWALD and BENG-LI

I believe we are part of a cosmic story that began before creation and which will continue long after we are forgotten. That puts our puny human arrogance in perspective. My son summed this up in a piece of art. It was a large green wheel on which was painted round and round the circle of the rim, 'On ... and on ... and on ...'

God marks no ending, only new beginnings,
until the consummation of our lives;
God keeps no count of losses, nor of winnings,
we move through grace, the holy spirit thrives.

So as we go beyond this time, this setting,
remembering all the laughter and the tears,
we go with God in faith, so not regretting
the moments shared, the hopes, the dreams, the fears.

Though parted for a while, we travel onward,
not knowing what the future has in store.
This phase will close, the spirit draws us forward,
we've tasted love, but God has promised more!

Metre: 11.10.11.10.

Suggested Tunes: LORD OF THE YEARS and O PERFECT LOVE

And here within the world, while we live, hope remains. Again and again God rebuilds, even when hope seems lost. There is no end to this cycle of opportunity and of renewal. So, after the most horrendous loss, we can ultimately feel hope, know love, reclaim praise. I am ready to launch off again into the future ...

Index of First Lines

First lines of choruses are shown in italic

Index of Printed Tunes

Index of Metres

Index of Themes

Biblical characters are shown in italic type

Index of Biblical References

Acknowledgements

The scripture quotations on pages 13, 15, 18, 107, 121, 124, 129 and 150 are from The New Revised Standard Version of the Bible, Anglicized Edition, copyright © 1989, 1995 by the Division of Christian Education of the National Council of the Churches of Christ in the United States of America, and are used by permission. All rights reserved.

The scripture quotation on page 59 is from *New English Bible* © Oxford University Press and Cambridge University Press 1961, 1970. Used by permission.

The phrase 'great prophet of pity' on page 93 is from Richard Holloway's book *Doubts and Loves* (Canongate Books, 2001) and is used by permission of the publisher.

The quotation on page 162 from Peter Storey's book *With God in the Crucible: Preaching Costly Discipleship* (Abingdon Press, 2002) is used by permission of the publisher.